Pope's Tree
Viper,
*Trimeresurus
popeorum*, is a
beautiful tree
(arboreal)
species noted
for its very
mild venom
and fairly even
temperament.
Photo by W.
Wuster.

VENOMOUS SNAKES
OF THE WORLD

TS—189

Facing page:
The King.
Perhaps the
most well-
known
venomous
snake in the
world is the
King Cobra,
*Ophiophagus
hannah.* Photo
by A. van den
Nieuwenhuizen.

1995 Edition

1   9 5

Distributed in the UNITED STATES to the Pet Trade by T.F.H. Publications, Inc., One T.F.H. Plaza, Neptune City, NJ 07753; distributed in the UNITED STATES to the Bookstore and Library Trade by National Book Network, Inc. 4720 Boston Way, Lanham MD 20706; in CANADA to the Pet Trade by H & L Pet Supplies Inc., 27 Kingston Crescent, Kitchener, Ontario N2B 2T6; Rolf C. Hagen Ltd., 3225 Sartelon Street, Montreal 382 Quebec; in CANADA to the Book Trade by Vanwell Publishing Ltd., 1 Northrup Crescent, St. Catharines, Ontario L2M 6P5 ; in ENGLAND by T.F.H. Publications, PO Box 15, Waterlooville PO7 6BQ; in AUSTRALIA AND THE SOUTH PACIFIC by T.F.H. (Australia), Pty. Ltd., Box 149, Brookvale 2100 N.S.W., Australia; in NEW ZEALAND by Brooklands Aquarium Ltd. 5 McGiven Drive, New Plymouth, RD1 New Zealand; in Japan by T.F.H. Publications, Japan—Jiro Tsuda, 10-12-3 Ohjidai, Sakura, Chiba 285, Japan; in SOUTH AFRICA by Lopis (Pty) Ltd., P.O. Box 39127, Booysens, 2016, Johannesburg, South Africa. Published by T.F.H. Publications, Inc.

MANUFACTURED IN THE UNITED STATES OF AMERICA
BY T.F.H. PUBLICATIONS, INC.

VENOMOUS SNAKES
OF THE WORLD

by W. P. Mara

With Short Contributions by:

Joseph T. Collins
Dr. Hobart M. Smith
Dr. Sherman A. Minton
Dr. Roger Conant
and
Dr. Henry S. Fitch

"...This book is dedicated to Lindsey Amanda,
who is and always will be
the motor that drives my inspirational machine,
and to Andy and Scott, two of the best and most
understanding friends an overzealous herpetologist
could ever have."

"...And of course, to my father..."

CONTENTS

Preface 6

Evolution, Classification,
  and Basic Morphology 11

Venom, Snakebite,
  and Venom Extraction 46

Acquiring Venomous Snakes 65

Proper Husbandry 82

Feeding 104

Reproduction and Captive Breeding .. 126

Sickness and Disease 141

Anecdotes
  Joseph T. Collins 159
  Dr. Hobart M. Smith 161
  Dr. Sherman A. Minton 165
  Dr. Roger Conant 168
  Dr. Henry S. Fitch 169
  W. P. Mara 172

Venomous Snakes and Man 174

A Few Interesting Species 181

Glossary of Terms 220

Further Sources 222

Index 223

PREFACE

The Yellow-jawed Lancehead, *Bothrops asper*, is a common ground-dwelling species ranging from Mexico south to South America, and grows to a length of up to eight feet. Photo by W. Wuster.

As an author of several books on the subject of herpetology, I can say I have spent quite some time involved in this field. But by "involved" I do not simply mean I have kept a lot of snakes or turtles. The hobby of herpetology consists of much more than filling a 10-gallon aquarium with gravel and a waterbowl, then placing a pair of ribbon snakes inside.

In fact, herpetology as an entity has so many facets that one could easily lose oneself in its intrigue forever. I know I certainly did.

Respectable field collecting, for example (or field "observing," you might say), is slowly becoming a popular pastime; and although this may have been spurred on by the dubious motives of a few greedy people who turned to Mother Nature for the sole purpose of financial gain, it is now transforming into a

wondrous, honorable hobby all its own.

Captive breeding as well, or as Joe Collins, herpetologist at the University of Kansas would say, "herpetoculturing," is also becoming a separate, living, breathing being. This is of course a wonderful thing, as it not only gives the hobbyist a chance to add first-rate specimens to his or her collection, but also takes a lot of pressure off the wild populations. This type of activity, as long as it is kept within reasonable, rational limits, should be supported at every turn.

Naturally there are a number of smaller, but still just as important, links in this huge chain (herpetological photography, for example), but the one we are going to be dealing with in the pages of this book is the investigation of an animal known throughout the world as the venomous snake. It will not be coverage of an intense, college-level nature, but simply a basic overview designed to give the reader a solid start.

Pareas margaritophorus, known in some circles as the Mountain Slug Snake, is an attractive opisthoglyph but difficult to maintain in captivity due to its dietary requirements. Photo by W. Wuster.

There are many topics involved in a subject like this. Most of these topics are covered to a certain degree, but thorough discussions, or perhaps the word "complete" would be better, would take up thousands of pages; I am just endeavoring to help you take the first step.

Most people who see the cover of this volume in passing will probably think: why on earth would someone write a book about a group of animals that no one would keep as pets in the first place? Wouldn't a book of that nature simply encourage that sort of thing?

No, it wouldn't. Books like these are not simply printed for the purpose of encouragement; they are printed for the purpose of learning. To enlighten those who are curious.

To help me in this quest, I have had the honor of being assisted by five of the most respected men in the field of herpetology, all of whom have contributed short stories to the anecdotal section. The value of their contributions is obvious:

Among the most popular venomous "hobby snakes" is Wagler's Pit Viper. As you can see by this stunning photo, the beautiful colors and pattern explain much of this popularity. Photo by A. van den Nieuwenhuizen.

Facing page:
A well-mounted cobra skeleton, exact species unknown. Photo by W. P. Mara.

they have all had such extensive experience in their profession (experience being perhaps the most priceless of all intangibles) that their tales cannot help but educate those who are less learned. My most sincere thanks go to this group.

I must also thank Dr. Herbert R. Axelrod, owner and father of TFH Publications, who gave me the opportunity to pen the book in the first place. A man who has done more to educate the minds of those interested in the pet hobby would simply be impossible to find.

Overall, this is not a "keeper's guide" to venomous snakes, but simply a reference manual for anyone who might be interested in the subject at hand. If in the long run that is the only purpose the reader feels it has served, then I say that is more than enough.

W. P. Mara

According to some sources, the horns of the Desert Horned Viper, *Cerastes cerastes*, have developed to keep sand and soil out of their eyes. Photo by C. Banks.

EVOLUTION, CLASSIFICATION, AND BASIC MORPHOLOGY

Until recently, all opisthoglyphs were placed in the subfamily *Boiginae*, based on the genus *Boiga*. Today many scientists doubt that this is a "real" subfamily. Shown is *Boiga multomaculata*. Photo by W. Wuster.

In this chapter the author will attempt to provide the basic knowledge needed to give the reader a solid foundation on which to further conceive his or her own studies on the topic of venomous snakes.

By primary definition, a reptile, of which of course a snake is, is an animal that has scales or horny plates rather than the simple skin that we as humans are familiar with, they breathe by way of lungs, and they are cold-blooded or poikilothermic, meaning quite simply that they cannot regulate their own body temperature, but must rely on the temperature of the immediate environment around them.

EVOLUTION

Snakes in general evolved during a time in the earth's history known as the Cretaceous Period some 80-85 million years ago (see chart below). There aren't many fossil records to go on, but those scientists that concern themselves with such things have worked up much evidence in support of this theory, so chances

are it is reasonably accurate.

GEOLOGIC TIME CHART
Recent Period (25,000 years ago-present)
Pleistocene Period (25,000-2 million)
Pliocene Period (2-12 million)
Miocene Period (12-30 million) *
Oligocene Period (30-40 million)
Eocene Period (40-60 million)
Paleocene Period (60-70 million)
Cretaceous Period (70-130 million)
Jurassic Period (130-168 million)
Triassic Period (168-200 million)

Snakes are those reptiles which, through millions of years of modification, have moved on from their ancestors, the lizards, by abandoning the usage of limbs (and thus losing the limbs themselves), having an eye with no lid, and "hearing" by feeling vibrations since they do not have external ears in the conventional sense.

Venomous snakes, which developed in a slightly different manner from non-venomous species, are those which have fangs or a set of enlarged teeth (of three basic types—which will

It is generally believed that the elapids, of which this *Micrurus dumerili* is an example, were the first venomous snakes to evolve, although other workers are convinced that this claim should be applied to the solenoglyphs. Photo by Robert S. Simmons.

*This was when the first venomous snakes, the elapids, were thought to have appeared.

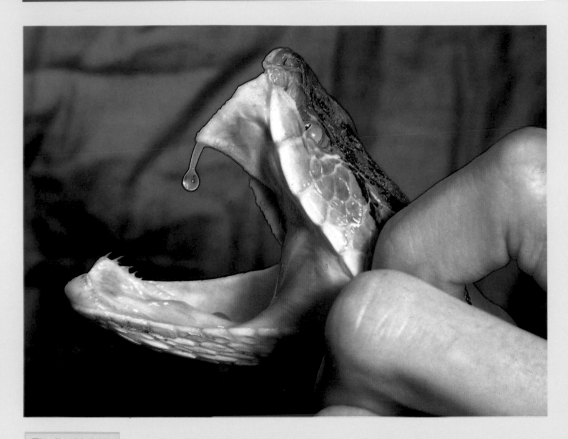

The liquid drop hanging from the fang tip of this *Agkistrodon* sp. gives a fairly good example of what most snake venoms look like. Photo by S. Kochetov.

Facing page: *Vipera xanthina* is a fairly typical example of a member of the Viperidae family. Note the diamond-shaped head. Photo by B. Kahl.

be discussed further on in this chapter), which can deliver a "poison" of sorts (in reality a very toxic form of saliva) for a multitude of purposes. The reader should keep in mind that in the technical sense, "poison" is something that is taken orally, and "venom" is something that is injected. Thus, if we are to walk the line of definition, to say a snake is "poisonous" is slightly inaccurate, but to say it is "venomous" is not.

The venom is produced directly in the venom gland from which it is secreted through a synthesizing process of certain enzymes. The reasoning behind why these modifications came about is rather detailed, but one can break it down into a series of simpler explanations.

For one, when snakes became snakes, they had some options, let's say: to alter their diet toward foods that were not as troublesome to secure (vegetable matter, fruits, etc.), or to continue on with their present preferences,

You can clearly see the fold of skin covering the fang on this Gaboon Viper, *Bitis gabonica*. Photo by Jim Merli.

which included a variety of living creatures that could put up resistance and thus make acquiring a meal more laborious. Since the latter obviously came about, and since the snakes were limbless, many had to find new ways of catching their prey.

Some became what we in the herpetological field know as "constrictors." Constrictors are those snakes which grab their prey with their jaws, wrap their bodies around the victim in a series of coils, and then suffocate them by means of powerful squeezing. The majority of larger non-venomous snakes overcome their prey this way, from 3-foot Fox Snakes to 25-foot Reticulated Pythons.

Then a second, slightly less common but still just as effective technique involves grabbing the item in the jaws and simply killing it either by sheer force of the jaws themselves or by grabbing and then pressing the item against another surface.

Today, members of the racer genus (*Coluber*) are good at this, as are the indigo snakes (*Drymarchon*). Interestingly enough, regardless of their size (both grow to well over 5 feet), neither have ever really developed the instinct to constrict, or perhaps they may have lost it over the course of time. Of course, most of the tinier snake species do not generally constrict either, but then their food items are usually so small they hardly have reason for such actions.

Finally, we have those snakes which take their prey by way of striking and then envenomating. These creatures developed their own special form of catching and consuming meals, and thus became very special themselves. The fangs that we are familiar with developed as a method of introducing digestive enzymes into the prey animals, thus helping speed up the digestive process.

They also came in useful when the need to ward off certain would-be aggressors arose. A popular misconception

The "sheaths," as the folds of skin covering a solenoglyph's fangs are called, will retract when the fangs puncture an object. Photo by K. H. Switak.

If nothing else, most venomous snakes can certainly be applauded for a varied diet. Here, *Bitis peringueyi* is seen taking a gecko, which is also a popular herpetological hobby animal. Photo by K. H. Switak.

about venomous serpents is that every time they strike they produce enough venom to kill whatever they are attacking, and that this is also done voluntarily.

In reality, many simply give what is known as a "warning strike," for the sole purpose of discouraging any further behavior on the part of the enemy who may or may not intentionally be irritating the snake in question. Sometimes the snakes do not even make contact! Scores of creatures, humans among them, have no doubt been granted continuation of their own lives through warning strikes. The author himself has seen multiple instances of snakes making contact with prey animals that would otherwise have easily succumbed to such actions, only to witness them continue on totally unhurt.

CLASSIFICATION

Somewhere around the mid to late 18th century, biologists from all parts of the world began to realize that

there were an incredibly large number of living creatures to contend with, and thus a system of classifying them in a way that could be used internationally had to be devised.

all living things were given a two-part Latin name; in fact, he even "latinized" his own name. The system of applying these names is known as "nomenclature," the

In 1758, Swedish botanist Karl von Linne (1707-1779), also known as Carolus Linneaus, published the 10th edition of his *Systema Naturae* in which he created a system of "binomial nomenclature" in which identification is known as "taxonomy," and the relationships are known as "systematics." These practices have grown considerably since their inception. At every level, they are based widely on morphological characteristics, both

Subspecies are sometimes named after particular people. This moccasin is known as *Agkistrodon bilineatus taylori*. Photo by R. T. Zappalorti.

The Red Diamond Rattlesnake gets its species name, *ruber*, from the Latin word "red." Photo by Ron Everhart.

internal and external, although exceptions do occur.

The arrangement therein involves a series of further classifications which go in order as follows: phylum, class, order, family, genus, and species. Of course, there are many "in-betweens" such as subspecies, subfamily, etc., but that branch of it is a bit too advanced for the confines of this book and therefore will not be explained.

Taxonomy is a practice that has caused many problems throughout the scientific field, mainly because many of its boundaries are very poorly-defined, plus there are a plethora of differing interpretations and philosophies as well as a multitude of new and erroneous observations. Names are constantly being juggled about, and such actions are consequently the cause for much confusion. Many workers tend to redescribe and redefine certain animals at the drop of a hat, and sometimes for the worst of reasons (personal recognition, etc.), but these kinds of problems

Sometimes subspecies names are created from the names of noted herpetological figures, like the Banded Rock Rattlesnake, *Crotalus lepidus klauberi*, named after Lawrence Klauber. Photo by S. Kochetov.

are to be expected with such a complex system and must be dealt with accordingly.

In the case of venomous snakes, the system is no different. Each is given a generic and specific rank (and sometimes a subspecific rank), and then summarily placed in another category, onwards up the ladder (or, as some people believe, down the ladder, because the species are the only "true" form of classification).

Interestingly, virtually all Latin names, although apparently nonsensical to the amateur, have very specific meanings, and

When a snake is listed with only a genus and species name, that usually means there are no subspecies, as in the case of this Green Cat Snake, *Boiga cyanea*. Photo by R. D. Bartlett.

logically correspond with the animals they are linked to. Very often these names are nothing more than the name of a scientist that has been latinized much in the same way Linne latinized his own name, but even then you can discern certain bits of information. *Agkistrodon piscivorus conanti*, for example, was named after the highly respected herpetologist Dr. Roger Conant.

In the interests of political correctness, when a Latin name is written out, the genus is capitalized and the following species and subspecies are not. Thus, *Ophiophagus hannah*, the King Cobra, is properly presented. The names of families, orders, etc., are also capitalized, although the words "family," and "order," etc., themselves are not.

MORPHOLOGY

For ease of understanding, this part will be broken down into three main sections, because morphologically speaking, there are three basic forms of poisonous snakes.

By definition, these are:

1) the solenoglyphs, those that have movable front fangs;

2) the proteroglyphs, those that have fixed front fangs;

3) and the opisthoglyphs, which are rear-fanged.

The author feels it would be much easier for the reader to grasp the morphological concepts of the venomous snakes by splitting them up this way rather than present them in a possibly more confusing "melting pot" type of format, and also to educate those who are less aware of the fact that there are indeed different "types" of venomous serpents, each with their own distinct and equally important features, rather than just classify them as those that have "big teeth"!

The Solenoglyphs

These snakes have often been regarded as the most advanced of the venomous species, due to the unusual and exclusive nature of their envenomating apparatus. They possess large fangs in the front

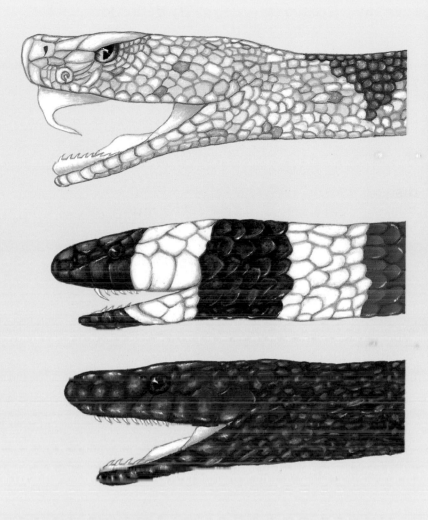

This illustration gives a good example of all three "types" of venomous snakes. From the top: a solenoglyph (front-fanged, movable), a proteroglyph (front-fanged, fixed), and an opisthoglyph (rear-fanged). Artwork by Alexandra Suchenko.

of their mouths, which can be seen on the upper jaw, and which fold into small cavities in the roof when the mouth is closed. Interestingly, the fangs can be operated independently of each other, although this is a skill not used all too often (except when "pulling" a prey item downward into the gullet). Another fascinating aspect of these fangs that many young hobbyists are unaware of is the fact that they are shed every now and then much in the same spirit a snake will shed its skin. New fangs of course replace the old ones, these coming from an area located on each side of the upper mouth just behind the current fang. Often one may notice,

Four examples of solenoglyphs. Clockwise from upper left: *Bitis gabonica rhinoceros*, *Trimerosurus albolabris*, *Atheris chloroechis*, and *Bothrops asper*. Photos by Robert T. Zappalorti, W. Wuster, Paul Freed, and W. Wuster, respectively.

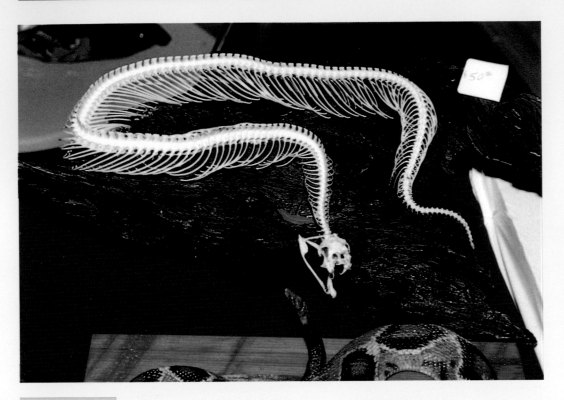

Notice the long ribs on this viper skeleton. Most members of the family Viperidae are fairly "husky" in girth. Photo by W. P. Mara.

while a solenoglyph yawns or strikes for its food, that there are actually two fangs present on one side (or sometimes even both sides) of the mouth. This is not at all uncommon, although admittedly it certainly looks unique. These are simply teeth which are in the process of being shed and replaced. The teeth themselves are usually longer than those that belong to snakes of the other two groups. They are moderately curved and of course hollow, with the discharge orifice being located just before the tooth point.

Another distinctive aspect of the solenoglyphs is not so much what equipment they have, but how they use it. The movable front-fanged snakes are, in general, perhaps the fastest-striking of all the venomous serpents. They don't "grab" as much as they "stab," and the motion is so quick that one could easily blink an eye and miss it. This action has developed so sharply over the course of time that the snake in question can lunge, strike, and resume the defensive posture in one smooth, swift movement long before the victim even realizes what has occurred.

Some of the more commonly known solenoglyph genera include *Crotalus*, *Agkistrodon*, *Bitis*, *Bothrops*, and *Trimeresurus*.

The Proteroglyphs

Perhaps the most outstanding feature of this group, apart from the obvious morphological characteristics we will discuss, is the fact that it contains some of the deadliest snakes in the world. Doubtless even the budding junior herpetologist has heard of the mambas, the cobras, and the coral snakes. These are all proteroglyphs, and should be avoided at every turn.

Proteroglyphs are morphologically unique in the sense that, unlike their front-fanged relatives the solenoglyphs, their fangs are generally smaller and basically fixed in place.

These teeth are not grooved, but rather they are hollow and canal-like, channeling the venom from the glands through what are known as ducts. In some species, these small fangs can actually move about slightly, in a rotary motion.

As some of you may already know, certain proteroglyphs have the small discharge orifice facing outward, and when the venom glands

Of all the venomous snakes, the Gaboon Viper, *Bitis gabonica*, holds the record for longest fangs. Some are over an inch and a half long. Photo by John Visser.

Four examples of proteroglyphs. Clockwise from upper left: *Elapsoidea sundevalli boulengeri*, *Naja naja kaouthia*, *Boulengerina annulata*, and *Aspidelaps lubricus*. Photos by Paul Freed, K. T. Nemuras, Aaron Norman, and Jim Merli, respectively.

saliva that seems to work wonders on their prey (primarily lizards) but which is basically ineffective on us.

Thus, mention should be made that although this grouping of serpents contains some very dangerous examples indeed (the Boomslang, *Dispholidus typus*, is certainly one; perhaps one of the deadliest snakes in the world in fact), the majority of opisthoglyphs are basically of no threat or consequence to man's overall health and/or safety.

An interesting morphological feature of the opisthoglyphs, at least internally, is the inclusion of something called the parotid, or, Duvernoy's gland. In basic terms, this is simply the venom-producing gland found in rear-fanged snakes, and was named after French anatomist D. M. Duvernoy. It is located in the roof of the mouth directly behind the supralabial gland, and contains an array of protein-secreting cells which aid in the breakdown of tissues in a prey item's body. It is

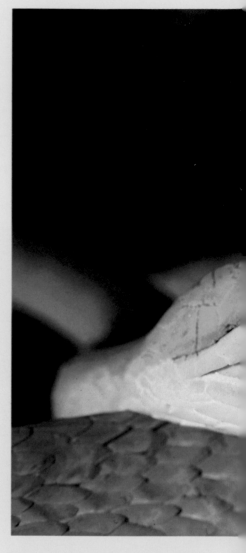

not necessarily unique, but simply less modified than the venom glands found in other species.

Those species that were discussed before which had enlarged teeth but were not considered dangerous, do not always possess the Duvernoy's gland. However, the explanation as to why

The vine snakes have never been terribly popular in the herpetological hobby, but they are rather unique-looking and make fair captives nevertheless. Photo of *Oxybelis fulgidus* by K. T. Nemuras.

they have the same effect on certain food items lies in the chemical makeup of their saliva. Without going into too much detail here, for that is beyond the scope of this particular chapter, suffice it to say that the salivary glands of certain "harmless" snakes have qualities which seem almost tailor-made to handicap items found only in those particular species' diets. Evolution indeed!

Some of the better-known genera in the opisthoglyph group include *Boiga*, *Telescopus*, *Chrysopelea*, *Psammophis*, *Leptodeira*, *Oxybelis*, and *Rhamphiophis*.

Four examples of opisthoglyphs. Clockwise from upper left: *Heterodon simus* (known in English as the Southern Hognose Snake, which, with its generic relatives, has been a favorite hobby pet for decades, many keepers never realizing that it is indeed a fanged snake), *Leptodeira septentrionalis*, *Dendrelaphis pictus*, and *Boiga ocellata*. Photos by R. T. Zappalorti, R. D. Bartlett, W. Wuster, and W. Wuster, respectively.

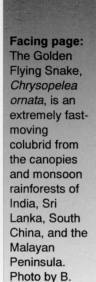

Facing page: The Golden Flying Snake, *Chrysopelea ornata*, is an extremely fast-moving colubrid from the canopies and monsoon rainforests of India, Sri Lanka, South China, and the Malayan Peninsula. Photo by B. Kahl.

A SHORT WORD ON THE FAMILIES

To the amateur herpetologist, most of the complexities involved in understanding systematics can be very confusing. When taking an overview of the subject, it must no doubt seem overwhelming. But if time is taken to try and understand the principles applied, you will no doubt realize that it really isn't terribly confusing at all, but instead largely a matter of memorization.

Thus the author does not feel it would be too out of place to add in a few short paragraphs explaining the venomous snakes in regard to families. Through this the reader will be able to gain a better understanding of the snake's relationships with members of their own family, as well as those of others. One final note worth mentioning is that the basis for the definitions offered here are purely traditional, although still currently utilized, but can change at any time and, judging by what has been progressing in the scientific community, probably will.

Family Colubridae

Generally speaking, this family constitutes what are often called "common snakes," and are furthermore regarded, somewhat erroneously, as "harmless" snakes.

While it is true that racers, bullsnakes, rat snakes, kingsnakes, and green snakes all belong to this family, so do the Boomslang, *Dispholidus typus*, and the Twig Snake, *Thelotornis kirtlandi*, both of which have been known to cause human fatalities. They are, as the reader has already learned, opisthoglyphs and carry with them some extremely virulent venom. The rear-fanged snakes belong to this family right along with those that do not possess such "equipment" (which are called aglyphs).

The separation of colubrids from other families is based largely on dentition (the structure and arrangement of the teeth). Colubrids can be active both day and

During the daytime, the Many-banded Krait, *Bungarus multicinctus*, is a calm, relaxed species, but when the night hours come, it becomes irascible and highly dangerous. This is fairly typical of many of the krait species. Photo by Dr. Sherman A. Minton.

night, and many have a very specialized diet (the Scarlet Snakes, *Cemophora coccinea*, for example, feeds almost exclusively on reptile eggs). They can be oviparous or viviparous, and haunt a wide variety of habitats. Some are terrestrial; others, like the Boomslang, are highly arboreal; and still others are devout burrowers. There are at present some 14 recognized subfamilies.

occurring in all the Americas, Africa, Asia, and Australia, the latter locale being its most "dominant" residency.

Most elapid venoms are neurotoxic, with a few hemotoxic qualities, and thus they are very dangerous. Elapids can occur terrestrially or arboreally, with a few being burrowers and a single genus, *Boulengerina*, being highly amphibious. Elapids can be either oviparous or viviparous, and these are both nocturnal and diurnal species.

Family Hydrophiidae

These are the sea snakes, and all are proteroglyphs. Many workers consider the sea snakes to be not so much an independent family in the standard sense but simply aquatic forms developed from the cobras and kraits. Generally speaking, hydrophiids are calm, peaceful creatures, but their venom is highly toxic. They do not make practical pets, and thus should not be sought. They are native to the Indo-Pacific and surrounding tropical

Family Elapidae

This family contains all the cobras and their allies, and thus all the proteroglyphs, save for the sea snakes in the family Hydrophiidae. Geographically, it is a very widespread family,

and subtropical seas. Sea snakes are strongly adapted to their environment and most have a prominent rudder-like tail and valvular nostrils. There is also a salt gland present in the jaws, this enabling salt excretion.

There are two subfamilies: Laticaudinae and Hydrophiinae, the former of which has to go on land in order to lay eggs; those in the latter subfamily give live

A juvenile specimen of Stoke's Sea Snake, *Astrotia stokesi*, this particular example amply displays what is one of the sea snakes' most distinct characteristics: the compressed tail. Photo by Dr. Sherman A. Minton.

birth in the water. In many areas, the meat and skin of sea snakes are traded commercially.

Family Viperidae

Perhaps the most interesting of all venomous snake families, Viperidae is made up largely by solenoglyphs. Traditionally, the family has been broken into two subfamilies: those snakes that have a heat-sensing pit ("pit" vipers) located between the eye and the nostril, and those that do not ("true" vipers). Several other minor groups are recognized today, and many workers question the validity of the pit as a true distinguishing character.

Most of the damage done to humans by members of this group is hemotoxic, though several species are at least partially neurotoxic as well.

Most viperids are nocturnal, hunting prey during the darker hours and then occasionally basking or seeking out mates during the day. Many will take to

burrows during the light hours. Others are highly arboreal.

A few are oviparous, but most give live birth. They range in a wide variety of habitats. Some having adapted to extremely non-reptilian surroundings (like the polar circle), while others are well-adapted to the rigors and trials of desert life.

They feed mostly on small mammals, and many do well in captivity although they never take kindly to human interaction and are best left untouched.

The rattlesnakes have long been popular in the herp hobby. Many of them do extremely well in captivity and come in a wide variety of colors and patterns. Photo of the Blacktail Rattlesnake, *Crotalus molossus*, by Ron Everhart.

VENOM, SNAKEBITE, AND VENOM EXTRACTION

Generally speaking, the one characteristic that separates the snakes outlined in this book from all others is that they are venomous. But what exactly is snake venom? What are its functions? Its chemical properties? Why do some venoms kill human beings almost reliably, while others do not? And do venoms have any beneficial qualities? These are some of the questions the author will attempt to answer in this chapter.

PROPERTIES OF SNAKE VENOM

Perhaps some of you have been fortunate enough to have seen, either in person, in a photograph, or on television, a professional herpetologist "milking" a venomous snake. If you watched carefully, and if the container the venom was running into was clear, you noticed that it appeared as a yellowish, pale-colored fluid. In some sea snakes, kraits, and the newborn young of a few species, venom is a little thinner and almost clear, but for the most part it appears in the yellow color mentioned previously.

Snake venom is a very complex mixture of chemicals called "enzymes," of which there are about 20 comprising all snake poisons worldwide. Although no venomous snake has all of these, the average number being between six and a full dozen, each enzyme has its own special function and effect. Some aid in the digestive process, others exist for the purpose of paralyzing prey. A few of the better-known chemicals and their believed purposes include: **cholinesterase** (found in most of the more dangerous species, particularly in the elapids), which attacks

The Tiger Snake, *Notechis scutatus*, is known to possess one of the most potent snake venoms in the world. Photo by Dr. Sherman A. Minton.

the nervous system, relaxing muscles to the point where the victim has very little control; **L-amino acid oxidase** (found in some vipers), which is responsible for the yellow coloring in that particular animal's venom, plus it plays a part in digestion and the triggering of other enzymes; **hyaluronidase** (found in many snake venoms), which causes other enzymes to be absorbed more rapidly by the victim; **proteinases** (commonly found in venoms of the family Viperidae), which play a large part in the digestive process of the snake in question, breaking down tissues at an accelerated rate (this is one of the enzymes that causes extensive tissue damage in human victims, as it is trying to help "digest" the flesh); **adenosine triphosphatase** (probably present in most snakes, certainly in most vipers), which is believed to be one of the central agents in the result of shock to the victim and an immobilizer for smaller prey; and **phosphodiesterase**

(also believed to be present in virtually all venomous snakes), which has accounted for negative cardiac reactions in victims, most notably a rapid drop in blood pressure.

These are but a portion of the overall makeup of snake venoms as they are known today. A few

other enzymes which have been isolated and identified are still a mystery as to what their exact purpose is, but as further research is done, more answers will undoubtedly come to light. Of course, since different species produce different reactions when they strike, it is both logical and correct to assume that the quantity of each of these toxins varies from snake to snake.

Elapids, for example, which contain a very lethal grouping of serpents including cobras, mambas, etc. obviously carry with them a much higher concentration of the more neurotoxic

Although regarded as a venomous species, the Copperhead, *Agkistrodon contortrix,* has very mild toxins and human fatalities almost never occur. Photo by R. T. Zappalorti.

The amount of damage inflicted on a human by a venomous snake varies from species to species. The Cottonmouth, *Agkistrodon piscivorus*, shown here, for example, is in the same genus as the Copperhead but usually causes much more tissue damage and unquestionably many more deaths. Photo by R. T. Zappalorti.

enzymes (neurotoxic meaning they affect the central nervous system, the brain, etc.). On the other hand, members of the family Viperidae have a notable concentration of hemotoxins (which affect tissues, muscle structure, etc.), thus causing a lot of scarring, gangrene, and permanent disuse of certain motory skills.

Of course, it is never as black and white as it may sound. Although Cottonmouths (*Agkistrodon piscivorus*) are vipers that mainly cause extensive destruction of the skin and muscle tissues, there are still the occasional deaths reported. By the same token, the author has seen some horrible skin damage on survivors of run-ins with cobras, mambas, and the like.

Finally, the popular question "which snake is the most venomous?" certainly carries with it a most general ring. Why? Simply because there is no one-dimensional answer.

For example, what do we mean by "most venomous?" Is that to ask, which has the most

venom, or which venom is the most toxic? There is a difference.

When they strike, all venomous snakes produce what is known as a "venom yield." This is a measurement (usually in milligrams) of exactly how much venom is produced in relation to how much is required for a lethal dose (a lethal dose is usually denoted as LD50 when referring to the amount needed to kill half the "recipients" in a study group—during clinical testing. These recipients are usually the standard mice and/or rats).

Some snakes contain venoms which are much more potent than others but do not produce as high a yield. The Eyelash Viper, *Bothrops schlegeli*, for example, has a yield of 10 20 mg, but their lethal dosage is around 15 mg (for a man, that is). But the Eastern Diamondback Rattlesnake, *Crotalus adamanteus*, a very deadly serpent, has an LD50 of 100 mg, and an average yield of between 300 and 500 mg. So you can see how much easier it would be for the rattler to terminate a human life.

But to be fair, and at least try to answer the original question, tests

If a hobbyist absolutely had to keep a venomous snake, he or she would be well-advised to make sure it was at least one that was not well-known for reliably causing human deaths. This Eyelash Viper, *Bothrops schlegeli*, is reported to be a good example of such a snake. Photo by Alex Kerstitch.

The Beaked Sea Snake, *Enhydrina schistosa*, is reputed to have the most virulent venom of all the world's serpents. Photo of a dead specimen by Dr. Sherman A. Minton.

tell us that the snake with the most toxic venom is the Beaked Sea Snake, *Enhydrina schistosa*, although certain vipers like the Gaboon Viper, *Bitis gabonica*, have an extremely high quantity yield (350-600 mg). So the answer depends on your perspective.

SNAKEBITE

No matter who the person in question is, one of the most dreaded fears of all herpetologists is being struck by a venomous snake. That fear is greatly justified. Let's face it—once you have been bitten, your very existence is in danger.

In this section of the chapter we will discuss and examine the many facets of snakebite, and hopefully the reader will glean enough information on the topic

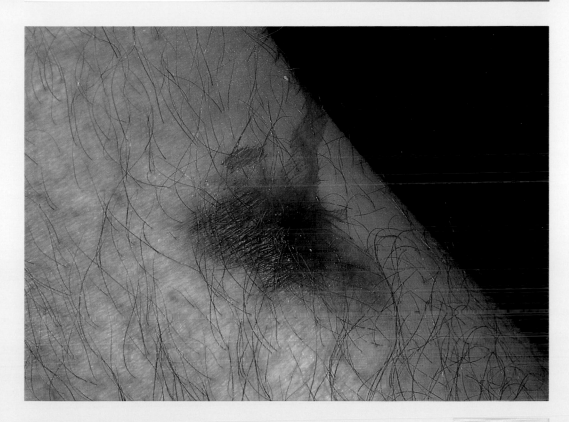

this way, rather than go through the agonizing experience of being bitten themselves.

A commonly asked question on the snakebite subject is, "How much of a snake's venom is released when it bites?" Many people assume that an average snake's venom gland is either so small that the carrier must empty it out completely or that they have no control over the output in the first place.

Both of those statements are incorrect. The truth of the matter is that the average percentage of venom released by a snake at any one time is somewhere around 10-20% of the total they are carrying at that given moment. Thus, it can be further stated with confidence that a venomous species will almost never release more than half of its current supply.

There are a lot of motions and operations at work during venom injection: the muscles that pressure the venom glands, the dropping down of the fangs, and then of course the actual strike and

Closeup of one puncture wound from a Copperhead bite. Note the localized discoloration of the tissues. Photo by Jim Merli.

ensuing contact itself. All of these procedures are voluntarily activated by the snake.

Furthermore, there are different "types" of strikes from different types of snakes. Vipers, for example, usually lunge out and strike quickly, then spring back into their original stance. Elapids (and occasionally rear-fangs as well) sometimes grab onto their prey and hold, even "chewing" every now and then. In the case of larger prey items, those which could easily drag the serpent around, this holding method is usually not performed, but overall, the vipers do not "grab" their prey at all, unless it is very small and easily managed.

The author supposes there are those who, regardless of the realization that snakebite is a very serious and life-threatening accident, are probably curious as to exactly how it feels to be struck. For the satisfaction of that curiosity, it will not be advised that anyone go out and taunt rattlesnakes or cobras

with their bare hands.

The author will, however, offer a few words on the subject by those who have already suffered through such experiences, and then perhaps you can make your own judgments from there.

Carl Kauffeld, one of the finest herpetologists who ever lived and

arguably the most skilled keeper, recalled being struck by a large cobra. In the book from which this story was taken (Sherman A. and Madge Rutherford Minton's *Venomous Reptiles*), he said that at first he felt nothing; no immediate swelling or localized burning (something more common with vipers). Then a mild "dopey" feeling and general weakening occurred, followed by a loss of alertness, resulting in a fuzzy darkness all around. He mentions being sure he was at least semiconscious during the entire incident, and that on the whole, at no

Survivors of cobra attacks claim that extreme physical pain is not something they suffered at the site of the bite. Photo of *Naja naja philippinensis* by Dr. Sherman A. Minton.

moment was it ever particularly painful.

From what we have learned about some of the more neurotoxic serpents, this story tells us much. It shows us how certain types of venoms do not so much "attack" a victim (attack being a word generally associated with painfulness), but more "affects" them.

Then, on the other hand, Dr. Henry S. Fitch gives a vivid account in his monumental book *Autecology of the Copperhead* of the time he jumped out of his car one dark night to try capturing an adult copperhead that had crossed the road in front of him and was heading for some bushes. While trying to pin its head down with a foot-long ruler (which was all he had available at the time), another car came around a bend some distance away and the headlights temporarily stunned him. The snake used this break in Dr. Fitch's concentration to its advantage, and turned and planted its fangs deep into the middle finger of his right hand, and then slid away.

He did not seek any immediate professional medical attention, but instead went home and began journaling his developing condition. He mentioned first suffering from an extreme burning sensation at the sight of the bite. Then the swelling began, and finally severe nausea and vomiting. Eventually he recovered and only a small scar remained.

This is a typical, and obviously unpleasant, scenario associated with a mild viper or pit viper bite. In some of the more extreme cases that the author is familiar with, such as with rattlers, adders, and so forth, there will also be a notable reaction in the cardiovascular system, resulting in time spent in a hospital. Other well known physiological reactions include sharp pains in the stomach and kidneys, numbness, and in cases left untreated, extensive gangrene.

Finally, a short note on the bites of rear-fanged colubrids. Although most of them are, as it was stated earlier, basically harmless, some can

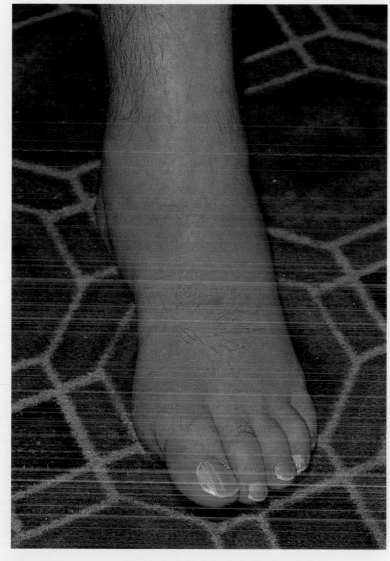

Localized swelling is one of many normal symptoms of Copperhead bites. Often, the area In question will double or even triple in size. Photo by Jim Merli.

cause very bad reactions and a few are almost dependably deadly. The most illustrative example of this is the death of noted herpetologist Karl P. Schmidt. In brief, he was handling a young Boomslang, *Dispholidus typus*, which promptly bit him on the thumb (this is not a terrible place to be bitten—the worst is on the neck, and the "safest" is on the buttocks). He sucked the wound as first aid, and then sought no further medical attention. The next day, he was dead. In some cases it may seem like a venomous snake has given a simple "warning strike,"

which many irritated venomous serpents often do (this is sometimes nothing more than a "bump" by the animal with its open jaws where no venom is injected. John Coborn, a somewhat prolific British author who has written many TFH books, had his life spared when an adder delivered a harmless strike to his face after he absentmindedly stuck his head into its tank while looking for a misplaced hammer. A further note on the saddening Karl Schmidt incident is that he felt no serious pains until about two hours before he succumbed. So as you can learn from this, any snakebite, no matter what the circumstances, should be treated with as much medical care as you can possibly give it.

Head study of the Boomslang, *Dispholidus typus*. Photo by R. T. Zappalorti.

IN THE EVENT THAT YOU ARE BITTEN...

Perhaps the most traumatic experience a keeper can endure is suffering an actual venomous snakebite. Depending on the species that has done the biting, the victim can expect anything from discomfort and mild tissue damage to the expectation of death.

The author does not wish to present a "plan of action" that presupposes any

information is given here in a simple list format and based on procedures that have been tested through use over the course of time.

1) The "official" course of action suggested most

assurance of recovery, since I am not a physician and thus do not wish to place my head on the proverbial chopping block. However, certain information can still be offered that will be helpful to anyone who has been bitten or feels they might be bitten in the future. This

often to those who have been bitten is: remain calm (this applies to both the patient and the aides); whichever extremity has been struck should be splinted and, if possible, placed in a dependent (below the heart level) position; physical activity should be reduced to the absolute

One of the most widespread of all venomous snakes is the Northern Viper, *Vipera berus*, which has caused more than its share of bites to humans. Photo by W. Wuster.

minimum, save for necessity; and the victim should be dispatched to a hospital immediately.

2) If you are housing venomous snakes, always keep the number of the nearest hospital clearly posted. If possible, place it in the memory bank of your telephone. Also, keep a map handy that has the route to the hospital clearly outlined, just in case someone has to drive you there. Finally, check to make sure the hospital in question carries the appropriate antivenom for the species you are housing.

3) For whatever it is worth, keep a "suction" extraction kit in your possession. These are commonly sold under various brand names in sporting goods stores and are relatively inexpensive, thus worth the money spent. Learn how to use this kit adeptly, as it may help save your life.

4) Do not handle venomous snakes without supervision, because in the event that you are struck, it is good to have another able body nearby to assist in making a phone call, driving a vehicle, administering some first aid, etc.

5) Finally, contact your physician and let him or her know you have a venomous snake in your possession.

In the lower part of this picture the reader can see one of the many products offered to aid in the treatment of a venomous snakebite. Photo by W. P. Mara.

Preventive measures such as labelling venomous snake tanks are without a doubt an excellent safety habit to get into. Photo by Dr. Fredric L. Frye, in *Reptile Care*.

They may be able to shed some valuable light on how your own particular body might react to a snakebite, and furthermore may be helpful to those at a hospital where you might be receiving treatment.

One last detail worth mentioning here is the use of a relatively new treatment involving electric shock. In short, a very small application of electricity (usually 20 kV, with 1 mA) is given at the sight of the wound. Most of the reports offered by those who have utilized this treatment (almost exclusively in the field thus far) have suggested that it is remarkably effective and the results almost "miraculous." However, at the time of writing there has been virtually no "actual" study (laboratory testing) done, and thus most academics are highly unwilling to endorse such a technique, at least until clinical studies have been made. Many field experts have considered this procedure "promising" and its potential worth investigating further.

VENOM EXTRACTION

The topic of venom extraction is certainly very fascinating to many people, mainly because most cannot possibly imagine something as dangerous as snake venom serving any actual useful purpose whatsoever.

But in reality, man has found many uses for the poisons that bubble within the

Facing page: Removing venom from a living snake is one of the most dangerous and unpredictable acts a herpetologist can perform. Photo of R. T. Zappalorti milking a Timber Rattlesnake, *Crotalus horridus*, by Peggy Vargas.

glands of the long, legless reptiles. Antivenom (also known as "antivenin") is one, the purpose of which is somewhat obvious if you simply pick the word apart. It is the "antidote" for many snake venoms. Unfortunately, antivenom usually has to be administered soon after a victim receives the bite or it is of no use at all. If you have been bitten somewhere far from the nearest hospital it is not going to be much help. Another drawback is that only certain kinds are available. It is a popular misconception that one antivenom suits all, but in fact each kind of snake must have its own particular antivenom. Although there are "polyvalent" antivenoms that can be utilized for certain "groups" of snakes related by chemical venom makeup, these are not always dependable either. You cannot, for example, treat a cobra bite with copperhead antivenom.

The most well-known method of producing antivenom is a technique referred to by many as the "horse serum" method. By this technique, a horse is injected with $\frac{1}{10}$ to $\frac{1}{100}$ of a lethal dose of venom, and this is increased slowly (usually during weekly intervals), until the horse can sustain about three or four times the lethal dosage. Blood is then taken from the animal and the serum containing the antibodies is then separated. Unfortunately, this is not totally foolproof either, as about one-third of all recipients have allergic reactions to horse serum. Standard procedure, in fact, calls for a test for serum sensitivity before giving antivenom.

The most common way of extracting venom is through the "milking" method. The fastest, although probably not safest, way of doing this is by taking the animal and forcing its fangs into the open mouth of a container, then, if the snake will not release any venom voluntarily (which happens often), pressing lightly on the venom glands (many people today use mild electric shocking

equipment). More often than not these containers will have thin membranes wrapped over the opening which the fangs will have to puncture. These are included to keep the extracted venom as safe from outside organisms as possible, and also to give the animal a feeling of "making contact" with something, which of course encourages venom secretion.

The venom is stored by deep freezing (sometimes with the help of a little liquid nitrogen) or drying. Unless kept extremely cold, fresh snake venom loses its potency very quickly. At room level temperatures and above, it loses virulency in about five minutes, but kept around -200°C it can be stored for up to thirty years, although a slight decrease in virulency under any circumstances will always occur.

The price for certain quantities of snake venom has been very high in the past (depending on the species and the amount needed), some high enough to purchase cars with! But when you learn that it takes about 400 snakes to produce the correct amount of dry extract, all of sudden the prospect of actually performing the duties involved seems very lukewarm at best. The author must stress here that many places in need of such venoms already receive them on a regular basis from reliable distributors, so please don't try milking on your own in the hopes of making a profit.

Finally, it is interesting to note that temperature not only affects venoms once they have been exposed to the air, but also causes changes in how much venom a snake will produce as well. During colder seasons, venomous snakes have very low production; during the warmer months, it hits its peak. This kind of knowledge is of great benefit to those who depend on a regular supply for pharmaceutical purposes.

ACQUIRING VENOMOUS SNAKES

Over the last decade, the Mangrove Snake, *Boiga dendrophila*, has become a highly regarded captive, and now many professional breeders include these on their regular price lists. Photo by B. Kahl.

As most hobbyists know, the process of acquiring snake specimens for the collection is generally not a difficult venture. For one reason or another, the hobby of herpetology has grown considerably over the course of the last decade, and as a result, many breeders have begun to appear, and

Although the Rough-scaled Bush Viper, *Atheris squamiger*, is not often seen in commercial herpetology, it is nevertheless an attractive serpent and does well on a diet of lizards and frogs. Photo by A van den Nieuwenhuizen.

many pet stores have expanded their herp sections considerably.

But where venomous species are concerned, the matter begins to get complicated, and for the obvious reasons. For one, some areas do not allow the collection and possession of venomous snakes, thus not only can the dealers themselves not sell them, but the hobbyists cannot have them to begin with. In such cases it is best to simply stick to the letter of the law, because the fines and penalties are usually quite severe.

For those who live in areas where it is permissible, however, there are a number of ways of acquiring venomous snakes. The two most common will be briefly discussed here.

COMMERCIAL PURCHASE

Even in localities where venomous species are allowed to be kept, it is rare to come across a pet store that will sell them. Thus, the author will not bother discussing such an eventuality but instead will concentrate more on the dealers and private breeders.

If you are in the market for a venomous snake, the most logical course of action to take would be to first get in touch with your local herp society or subscribe to either its journal or one of the popular magazines. This will at least put you in touch with people who have, or know those who have, bred venomous snakes.

Of course, at this point you should already have some idea of what snake you are after. If you do not, then perhaps browsing through the species section of this book will help. If that does not suffice, there are many other books with appropriate photos and text. Keep in mind that you as a potential keeper will have your limits, some of these being cost, space, and commercial availability of the species.

The latter point, for example, is one that should be of particular interest. After you have found a suitable source, you must then inquire as to whether or not they have the particular animal you are looking

Facing page: If you are brave enough, you can always turn to Mother Nature for venomous snake specimens. On the top is an example of dry, pine woodlands, a good place for many burrowing species. On the bottom is an example of a small litter pile. Both photos by W. P. Mara.

for. You may be disappointed, as most species are simply not very popular and thus not very profitable. But there are still many venomous snakes being bred currently in captivity that would appease an interested party. Once you have located one, the next step is to then get it physically into your possession.

If the seller you are dealing with is not from your immediate area, chances are you are going to have to have the animal shipped. This can be somewhat expensive. Laws concerning the shipping of venomous snakes often are very explicit and the penalties for violating those laws extremely harsh. Chances are you are going to have to do a bit of research to find out all the specific answers to this matter, but transactions like these are made from time to time, so it is not completely impossible.

Once you have the snake in your possession (and are absolutely assured that the container it is in is completely secure),

bring it to its new home and quarantine it immediately. Observe it closely for the next two weeks to make sure it has not fallen victim to any illnesses. Many reptile ailments, like the vicious Fer-de-Lance Virus described later on, are highly contagious, so care should be taken to assure the animal's health before placing it in with your other pets.

WILD COLLECTING

The second most common way of acquiring a venomous snake is by going into the wild and locating one yourself. This is where limits fall heavily into play, because if the species you're looking for is not native to your area, you're out of luck. And don't forget that even venomous snakes become endangered and are consequently placed on many governmental protection lists. Go to the trouble of finding out if what you are doing is even legal in the first place.

Once you have consulted a reliable field guide and discovered a local snake that piques your interest, you must then go about finding it

Rocky, wooded areas are first-rate habitats for venomous snakes. Photo by Dr. Herbert R. Axelrod.

in a rational, sensible manner. You are not going on "the hunt" in the traditional, romantic sense. Many venomous snakes are capable of killing and no one is immune to that possibility. There are some common guidelines that can be followed.

For one, it is very ill-advised to try and look for a venomous snake on your own. In the event that you are bitten, you will simply need help.

Secondly, it is wise to wear not only a pair of thick jeans or similar heavy pants, but a pair of thick leather boots as well. This will of course lower the odds of a snake's fangs actually making contact with your skin in the event that you are struck.

Do not use your bare hands when searching under brush, logs, rocks, or debris, but instead invest in a long hoe or something similar and let the implement do the work. The idea is to minimize the amount of interaction you have with the surrounding environment.

Finally, if and when you do come across the animal you are seeking, place it in a bag with a grabstick (otherwise known to many as a "pilstrom tongs"), rather than by hand. The reasons for this are so obvious as to not even warrant explanation. You won't be impressing anyone by grabbing a poisonous snake, you'll just be endangering lives.

When carrying your find back to the car, house, etc. remember to always keep the bag well away from your body and make sure it is secure. Snakes have a nasty habit of pressing on weakly knotted bags

Many venomous species use the crevices in rocky hillsides for both hibernating purposes and as an effective escape from predators. Photo by Dr. Herbert R. Axelrod.

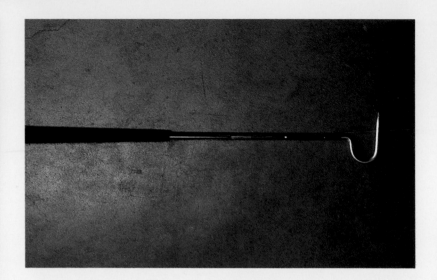

A simple snake hook, usually used in conjunction with a "grabstick." Photo by Dr. Fredric L. Frye, in *Reptile Care*.

to the point where they simply unravel, and while this might be amusing to those who hunt tiny ringneck snakes, with rattlers and adders the humor is definitely decreased.

A BRIEF NOTE ON EQUIPMENT FOR HANDLING

There are some times during the course of keeping venomous snakes when they will have to be physically manipulated to some degree. Fortunately, there are many items available on the herpetological market designed for just this purpose.

One is the grabstick, or tongs. In essence, this is simply a long (about three to six feet), usually aluminum, stick with a handle at one end and a pair of tong-like "fingers" at the other. The nice thing about these is that you can judge how much pressure is being put on the animal. They are relatively inexpensive, and can be obtained primarily through mail-order.

Another essential tool is the snake stick. Snake sticks look more or less like golf clubs without the club end, and the tip of the pole opposite the handle bent at a 90° angle. They come in a variety of sizes and are relatively cheap. These of course are a little harder to handle than the grabsticks, but then many venomous snakes, as long as they are lifted at midbody, do

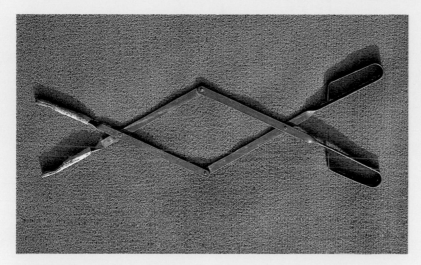

A device less used are these "zigzag" tongs. It is not very effective in confined spaces and does not permit the user the liberty of accurate pressure judgement. Photo by Dr. Fredric L. Frye, in *Reptile Care*.

not really seem to mind the movement anyway. Pinning down a head with a snake stick is certainly a lot easier than it is with a grabstick.

Again, it should be stressed that there are obviously many better ways to handle a venomous snake than with one's hands, so do yourself a favor and use a tool of some kind.

They are certainly more disposable than you.

A FEW COMMENTS ON VENOMOIDS

Question: Would you keep a King Cobra or a Boomslang if it could be rendered harmless?

The basic idea behind that statement is one of the hottest topics floating around the herpetological hobby right now. There

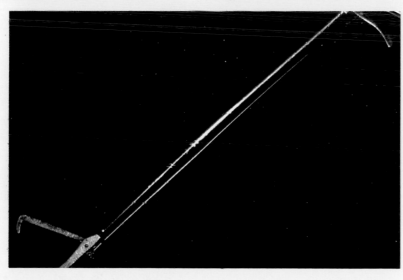

The "grabstick" is probably the most commonly used implement today in the manipulation of venomous snakes. Photo by Dr. Fredric L. Frye, in *Reptile Care*.

Facing page: Rattlesnakes like these *Crotalus mitchelli* are among the most often utilized "victims" of the venomoid craze. Photo by Ron Everhart.

probably has been no subject more controversial than the progress of the venomoids.

By definition, venomoids are venomous snakes which, through the deliberate actions of man, have been made "safe." This involves the execution of a delicate surgical procedure, of which there are two main types: that in which the animal's venom glands are removed completely (usually done with the assistance of a laser), and that in which the animal's ducts are severed, thus cancelling the flow of venom to the fangs. In the latter the venom is still produced, though.

Through this modern "miracle," a hobbyist could conceivably own just about any snake that would normally be considered "dangerous," in a fashion where it would harm no one, save for the occasional puncture wounds given by the remaining fangs (which, incidentally, should never be removed, since experience has shown that "defanged"

venomous snakes feel "unarmed" and are consequently too scared to touch food, thus of course leading to a swift health deterioration and ensuing death).

Although relatively new to the herpetological hobby, venomoids have in fact existed for quite some time. They have been used for various scientific research projects, as well as for display purposes in many zoos. They are obviously much safer to have around, and thus more practical.

Many people have presented concerns about the physical health of such snakes. It has been suggested that venomoids do not live full lives, that they do not eat well due to their removed "apparatus," and that some will in fact not eat at all, and thus begin the long spiral downward that eventually leads to death.

But the fact of the matter is that many professionals who have kept venomoids for valid purposes have insisted that these concerns are basically unfounded.

They report that "venomless" snakes kept in their care have lived normally and without decreased longevity.

That is not to say there aren't any notable changes in a venomoid's behavior. Although the author has only seen a handful of venomoid snakes, he has not ventured to hold any in his own hands, but has heard a multitude of reports from those who have that they are remarkably calmer than one would expect from that particular species. There was one man, in fact, who had a large Indian Cobra which he repeatedly encouraged to strike, but which would not.

Furthermore, venomoids seem to grow and eat as normally as any other captive snake would, provided of course they are given normal, attentive treatment. Many keepers of venomoids feed their stock pre-killed food by way of forceps, and eventually will simply leave the food item in the cage. Apparently all species respond to these actions and feed regularly without fuss.

But the author does not wish to present only the positive side of the venomoid issue. In fact, I do not wish to take a side on this issue at all (I naturally have my own opinions, but this book is not the appropriate place to spotlight them). Instead, I will present all the facts and let you, the reader, decide for yourself.

The cobras are possibly the most commonly seen venomoid snakes. Photo of a *Naja naja sumatrana* by M. J. Cox.

On the down side, some say venomoids are bad for the hobby, and that once there have been a few unfortunate "accidents," many local governments may get fed up and ban the keeping of snakes entirely.

Another excellent point to be considered is the fact the venomoids are alarmingly misleading in the educating of children. How many youngsters are going to see someone free-handling a rattlesnake or a cobra without the desperately needed knowledge that those particular animals are "unique" and thus do not reflect the actual dangers involved? What would they then do later on when they come across one in the woods near their backyard?

Additionally, how can a buyer be sure the snake he or she is getting is indeed a venomoid? It would be very easy for a seller to "slip up" and accidentally mix up a venomoid with a truly "hot" snake. What happens when the unfortunate buyer drops dead after being bitten? This is not to say a seller would do this on purpose, but whether on purpose or not, once a hobbyist becomes a victim, the damage has already been done.

Do not forget either that just because a snake has no venom output does not mean it cannot harm you. Deep puncture wounds can be very painful and easily lead to further infection. Salmonella, a very unpleasant disease carried by many herpetiles, can be transimitted through a wound of this sort, as can other infections. Venomoids with glands intact may be able to release saliva even with the ducts cut.

Finally, it would not be too obvious to state here that two venomoids will not produce more venomoids; they will produce young just as deadly as their parents are "supposed" to be. This too, I think, will be a major downfall in the keeping of venomoids.

This issue is obviously one that needs much further thought and consideration. As I stated earlier, I do not wish to take a stance on the subject, but simply present arguments from both sides. Ultimately only you, the keeper, can make the final decision.

PROPER HUSBANDRY

Before we go further into this chapter, I would like to write a general disclaimer which says, in short, that I do not in any way agree with the concept of keeping venomous serpents in the home or any other type of domestic scenario, nor do I encourage it. The plain fact of the matter is that the practice of keeping venomous snakes is, to put it simply, much too dangerous and consequently cannot be recommended for the average hobbyist. Even those who consider themselves "professionals" are

Clearly labelling a venomous snake's tank (and including a warning symbol like the one shown here) is an absolute must. Photo by Dr. Fredric L. Frye, in *Reptile Care*.

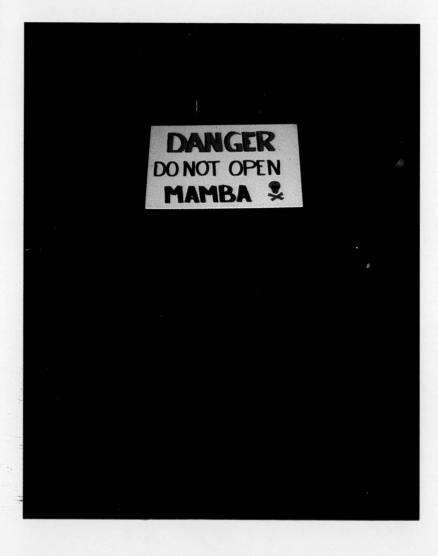

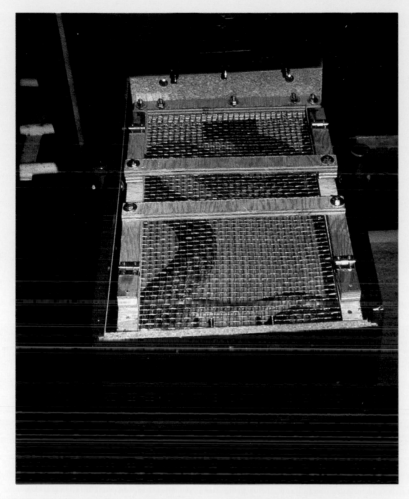

A top made with hardware cloth might be okay for temporary quarters, but in the long run a venomous snake should be kept in much "tighter" accommodations. Photo by Dr. Fredric L. Frye, in *Reptile Care*.

always at risk, so I feel it is my duty to serve as a voice for the majority of those who may be labelled responsible for the accurate and rational conveying of dependable information to those who wish to be enlightened. Having said that, I can now move forward in this section.

HOUSING

Perhaps the most vital consideration in the keeping of any potentially dangerous animal is proper housing. It would probably be more accurate to state that as "secure" housing, but those two ideals of course go hand in hand.

Generally speaking, venomous snakes are somewhat relaxed in their day-to-day behavior. At least North American species seem to be this way. The copperheads (*Agkistrodon contortrix*),

Organic substrates like crushed bark are ideal for snakes. Most organic substrates are easy to work with, pleasing to the eye, and can be bought in bulk quantities. Photo courtesy of Four Paws.

for example, can sit for hours in the exact same position, unmoving and perfectly content. A few other varieties show this type of behavior as well (Gaboon Vipers, *Bitis gabonica*, for one), and this tells the keeper something about housing requirements.

As we know, most

chart below will let the keeper know what size tank he or she will most likely need. This is, of course, assuming that the herpetologist in question does not have a problem with using a commercial all-glass aquarium rather than building one from scratch.

snakes like to have room. Many species prefer, as you would expect of all livings things, never to be too cramped. However, that preference is not quite as severe in venomous snakes. Size of the cage is an important consideration, as is its shape.

To make matters as simple as possible, a

Snake Length	Tank Size
Up to 2 feet	10 gallon
3-6 ft.	20 gal.
7-10 ft.	30 gal.
over 10 ft.	55 gal.

Glass aquariums, which are perfectly suitable for keeping venomous species, can be found in the pet shops. They are infinitely better than homemade tanks, since

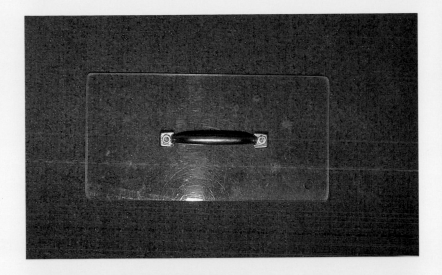

If you must usc hardware cloth on your top, at least have a clear plastic "cover" with a handle on it when working in close quarters. All photos by Dr. Fredric L. Frye, in *Reptile Care.*

Under-tank heating pads work well with most snakes. A keeper can warm only one particular section of the enclosure, giving the inmate more than one temperature zone to chose from. Photo courtesy of Hagen.

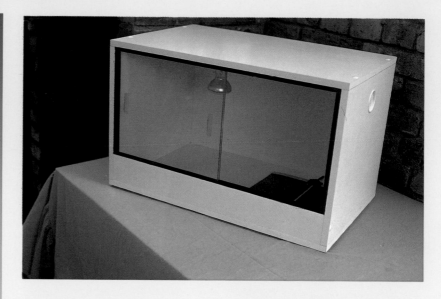

If you want to take the time, and if you have a little bit of carpentry skill, you can always build your own tank. The one depicted in this photograph is acceptable for venomous species, provided the front pieces can be locked. Photo by Susan C. and Hugh Miller.

most of these are generally not as safe. Many are made from wood, which of course can swell and shrink depending on the temperature, humidity, etc. not to mention that they can warp, leaving large gaps. Finally, quite a few are constructed with a large quantity of hardware cloth, which of course is totally inadequate when trying to hold venomous serpents. Even if an eager hobbyist decides to go as far as to use plexiglass for viewing purposes, the expense of this becomes so great after a while that the cost will surpass that of a glass tank in the first place, so why bother? Overall, it is advised

that the keeper stick with commercially-bought all-glass aquariums. Make sure the one you buy has glass thick enough to avoid the possibility of an occupant smashing through it (while chasing prey, striking at passersby, etc.) and getting loose.

For your own peace of mind, do not rest a glass tank containing a venomous serpent on any surface that isn't completely steady. A shaky, weak-legged table or a shelf that is too shallow could very easily result in a keeper coming home one day only to find a scattering of shattered glass on the floor and a venomous, maybe even deadly, snake roaming about—

somewhere. The possible end results of such a mishap are too terrifying and grisly to contemplate; especially if children are involved. (It goes without saying that people who keep venomous animals in the same house with children are a little crazy to begin with.)

Tank Tops

As far as general security measures with glass tanks are concerned, the top is obviously the most important feature. Tops are available in quite a variety of styles, but the best ones are those that provide adequate ventilation while not giving the animal in question enough space to stick a fang through or squirt some venom from.

Mesh-type screening, even the tougher varieties, is almost good enough, but almost is not what the keeper wants. This type of top can tend to be somewhat weak and easy to puncture. Perhaps with some of the smaller species it is acceptable, and of course the young of many of the larger ones, but beyond that, not really.

Another commonly seen unacceptable tank top is made primarily of quarter-inch hardware cloth. Although these are more than adequate for harmless snakes, there is certainly enough room in the screening itself for a poisonous snake to slip a fang through, embedding it into the finger of some unfortunate soul.

Thus, the keeper is left with one other option: construct your own top. If you decide to choose this route, use either eighth-inch hardware cloth (it may be harder to find and a little bit more expensive, but it is the perfect medium between fine mesh and quarter-inch) or simply make a solid wood top and drill about six one-inch holes in it, covering these on **both sides** of the wood with strong wire mesh.

In either case, whether you decide to just go ahead and purchase a top or build one from scratch, the most important consideration is to be absolutely sure it can be locked on firmly. Many

For some of the more heavy-bodied serpents, like this Russell's Viper, *Vipera russelli*, you will have to take into consideration the possibility of using fairly thick glass. Photo by Ron Everhart.

keepers seem to forget one of the snake's most enduring characteristics: its Houdiniesque knack for getting out of many apparently escape-proof confines.

For the purpose of securing lids you have a few options at your disposal, but the one discussed here is the most popular and probably the most reliable as well. It is nothing more than a small metal clip, and can be bought (or at least ordered) in pairs at most herp-oriented pet shops. It comes in two general styles: circular and rectangular. The basic idea is that one is attached to each side of the tank, just under the plastic border, and then along the edge of the top itself. Of course, if you decide to build your own top you must modify the edges to accommodate these clips. This can be done very easily in a number of ways; all you really need is a little bit of carpentry skill and some common sense ingenuity.

One final suggestion on the top-clip issue that the author feels should be mentioned is that it's an excellent idea to buy not one, but two sets of clips (totaling four) for each cage you intend to use. These would then be placed on all four sides of the tank, thus adding an extra measure of security to the situation. In the long and short of it, it is certainly more sane to spend the extra cash if the final result is going to be double the security.

Keep in mind that many places require by law that the keeper not only have his or her venomous snake tanks locked, but also that the "snake room" be locked as well, with signs clearly posted on the doors as to the nature of what's inside, so in those cases clips will not be sufficient anyway. Furthermore, along the same lines, some places require you to be insured and bonded before you can even keep venomous animals, and most homeowners insurance policies do not cover bites by venomous snakes. It is very wise and strongly advised that you check with your relevant government agencies

Since snakes have a tendency to turn a nicely arranged tank into utter chaos, it is best to decorate a venomous species's tank as simply as possible. Photo by Jim Merli.

and make absolutely sure you know your corresponding laws before going one step further. In some locations, the fines for violating such rules can be quite severe.

Cage Decor and Shiftboxes

It seems almost pointless to bother with a section on decorating the cage of a poisonous snake, since, as most experienced hobbyists know, in order to keep a nicely arranged tank looking good you must give it a fair share of attention—and who wants to stick their hands into a rattlesnake's tank just to put the fake tree branch back in its upright position?

Therefore, the author has decided to sidestep the problem entirely and encourage an absolute minimum usage of cage decoration to begin with. In short, this means things like real plants, elaborate water containers, and natural substrates are basically out, replaced by simpler, although visually more clinical, additives (unless for some reason they are absolutely necessary).

For example, the substrate. Since this is usually the one item in a snake's cage that gets soiled most often—and thus has to be changed

If you do not wish to place a shiftbox into the tank itself, you will have to "guide" your animal into an external one. Photo by Jim Merli.

most often—you are certainly not going to provide a venomous serpent with a bedding that is so intensely detailed that you find yourself pulling everything out of the tank and scrubbing it clean every other day. For those who keep venomous snakes, the entire cleaning process must be as quick and trouble-free as possible. For this purpose, simple paper towels (soft and uncolored) are probably best. They are inexpensive, completely disposable, easy to work with, and safe and clean enough to bed a cage with at all times without suffering the traditional worries of mite infestation, germ warfare, etc., that you get with other substrates. Of course, you may run into those species whose bedding requirements are so unique that paper towels simply will not do, but even in those cases the key word to remember is simplicity, because good husbandry involves constant attention to cleanliness.

Another cage items to be concerned with is a

In the author's opinion, it is better to place the shiftbox directly into the tank, thereby reducing the risk of accidents. Photo by Jim Merli.

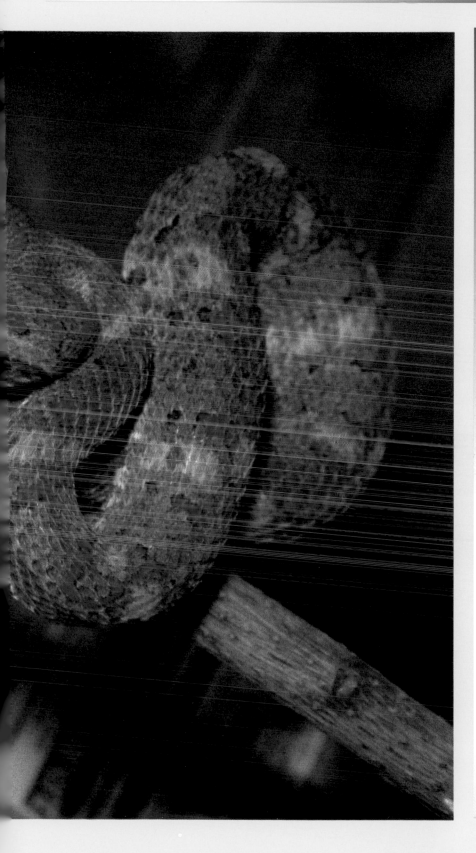

If you look closely, you will see that the floor of this Eyelash Viper's, *Bothrops schlegeli*, tank is bedded simply with newspaper. This is an ideal substrate for venomous species. Photo by J. T. Kellnhauser

waterbowl, which should be larger on the bottom than at the top so it cannot be tipped. Beware of those that have hollow bottoms. Many a keeper has received quite a surprise by lifting one of these only to find a tiny serpent hiding underneath. Provide a branch or two only in the event that the snake in question is very arboreal and would be considerably more miserable without one (this of course would demand a higher-style tank, which can also be purchased or ordered at any well-stocked pet store). Also remember to put in a rock or a stone (with only a slightly abrasive surface) to aid in shedding (again, beware of hiders).

Finally, and perhaps most importantly, the cage must have a "shiftbox" in place of the more conventional "hidebox" seen with the harmless species. When one considers the fact that any captive animal, no matter what it may be, will have to be removed from its place of residence from time to time, it becomes obvious that the need

for a reliable method of removal is imperative. Naturally, in the case of venomous snakes, the seriousness of this priority increases tenfold. Therefore, the author would like to suggest a time-tested method that is about as safe as safe can be in a situation such as this.

The central idea behind the shiftbox is, quite simply, a hidebox with a front door that can be locked from the outside, sealed to the point where the prisoner within is not in touch with the outside in any way.

Since I know of no shiftboxes offered with any degree of commercial regularity, it becomes necessary for the hobbyist to build his or her own. This can be done with some wood, a few simple tools, and rudimentary knowledge of carpentry. The exact details of the matter will not be explained, as doubtless the size and style of the container will vary from species to species, as well as from hobbyist to hobbyist, but the essential idea remains consistent: what you are trying to do is create a box that

Keeping an eye on your snake's ambient temperature is an important facet of good husbandry. If the animal is allowed to become too warm or too cold, it could become ill. Fortunately, high-range thermometers designed specifically for herp-keeping are now available. Photo courtesy of Hagen.

can be safely shut and locked after the serpent has been "chased" inside. The box must be sturdy, it must not have any openings whatsoever, and most crucially, the "door" must be utterly reliable, since one can easily imagine the obvious misfortunes that would result if the front popped open while the box was being removed, leaving a very angry cobra or cottonmouth staring you in the face.

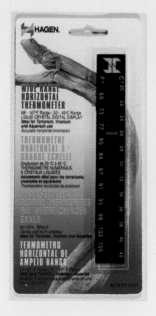

Lighting

Some hobbyists, at least those who are familiar with the husbandry of both lizards and turtles, may be aware of the concepts behind proper lighting in the reptile or amphibian aquarium. The theory is that lizards and turtles need full-spectrum lighting, which takes the place of actual sunlight, in order to thrive, whereas snakes and frogs, etc., generally do not. However, the point should be made that if you are planning on breeding your stock, venomous or otherwise, full-spectrum light should be used regularly. Special bulbs designed for just this purpose can be obtained at your local pet store and are highly recommended by the author.

The second function that lighting serves is called the provision of a "photoperiod," which simply means the amount of "daylight" an animal receives. Although a seemingly subtle detail, photoperiods tell a snake things like what

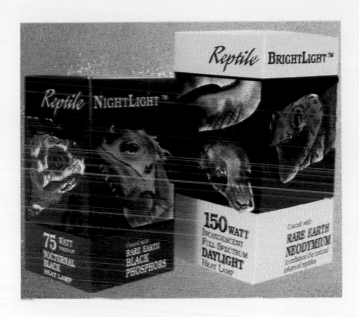

season it is (along with temperature, etc.), and this of course has an effect on their overall behavior.

Generally, it is best to provide your captive with the photoperiods they would be experiencing in their natural environment. Thus, if you were keeping a Timber Rattler (*Crotalus horridus*) and it was midsummer, you would keep the lights on for about twelve to fifteen hours each day.

In the fall, the day would of course get shorter. If you do not pay attention to this function, you could confuse an animal very badly and run the risk of it not breeding for you at all.

Heating

Since venomous snakes are cold-blooded, they must rely on whatever heat source is nearby to warm them. In captivity, the provision of that source is solely up to the keeper.

Facing page:
Using a clear plastic barrier is a fairly reliable method for keeping venomous snakes at bay while their waterbowls are being removed for cleaning. Both photos by Jim Merli.

One of the most popular methods is by use of what is called a "hot rock" or "heat stone." This is a small, commercially available item that looks more or less like a simple terrarium stone, but has a cord running out of it which connects to a standard socket and provides about 85°F-90°F of radiant heat. One nice thing about the "hot rock" is that a snake can avoid it when it wants to. The down side is that an opening in the tank itself or its cover must be made for the cord to run through, and that of course takes away from security.

A second technique is the use of what are called spot lamps or heat lamps. These too can be avoided by the occupant if it wishes, but again, you must leave room for the wiring if the lamp is actually placed into the cage.

Finally, probably the most efficient way to provide heat without sacrificing security is to simply run a small heater in the room itself, regulating the temperature by way of a thermostat. Many models are now available that have built-in regulators, and some are actually rather inexpensive. The ceramic varieties are probably the most merciful on your electric bill, certainly another consideration to keep in mind.

Humidity

A final climatic consideration is humidity. Again, the line of logic to follow there is to go with what is dictated by the animal's natural environment. The keeper can provide humidity a number of ways, but the easiest is to simply mist the inside of the cage on a regular basis. This can be done safely by aiming a misting bottle through the air holes, being careful not to mist the snake itself. With a reasonable temperature of water this generally will not harm them, but be careful not to spray into their face, as this will certainly irritate them beyond belief.

Tank Cleaning

So now that you have read through the general concepts behind tanks and most

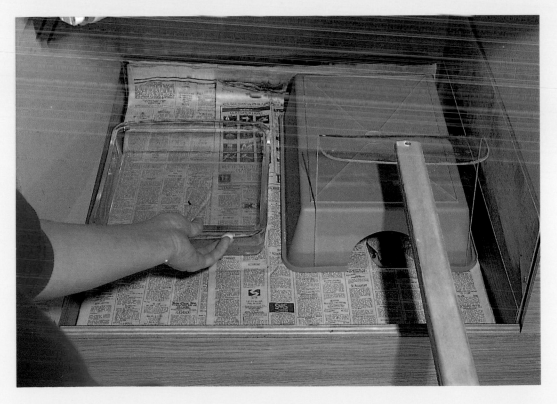

Providing your snakes with the correct photoperiod (day/night cycle) is very important. Photoperiod is often a factor in determining a herptile's behaviorisms. Bulbs designed specifically for the keeping of reptiles and amphibians now are available at many pet shops. Photo courtesy of Energy Savers.

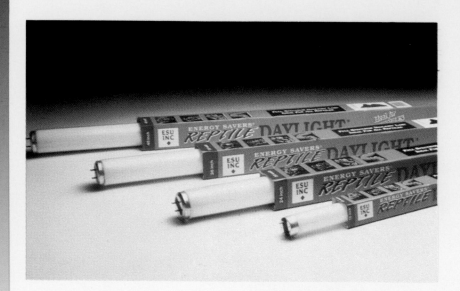

importantly how to contain the occupants, the final lesson in housing is how to clean them.

Let's say for the sake of argument that your snake has already been encouraged into its shiftbox and the front has been completely secured. Remove the box and place it in yet another closeable container (a bucket with a lid, for example) for added safety.

Now that the animal is properly confined, you can clean the tank as you would any other reptile terrarium. A

simple method the author has utilized repeatedly with much success is outlined below:

1) Remove all cage items and either dispose of them or wash them with warm, soapy water (liquid dish soap is mild enough, but things like laundry detergent soaps are quite dangerous) and bleach (10 to 1 mixture), then rinse thoroughly in cold water.

2) Fill tank about to one quarter with the same cleaning mixture, scrub all sections vigorously (especially

corners), and rinse thoroughly, also with cold water.

3) Replace all decor items, then replace shiftbox and carefully release occupant.

This is a literally worry-free technique that is both easy and reliable for the destruction of germs. A good, careful cleaning of this kind should be practiced at least every fortnight, but ideally once every week.

An opaque eye is a sign that a snake is about to shed, and thus will not take kindly to any form of handling. Photo of *Crotalus adamanteus* by Jim Merli.

FEEDING

Frogs are a small but significant part of many venomous snakes's diets. Photo of *Naja* sp. taking a frog by A. van den Nieuwenhuizen.

The issue of feeding is, in the author's opinion, the most important facet of actually keeping a snake, whether it is venomous or not, in peak health. The plain truth of the matter is that you as the keeper have command over every other aspect of husbandry (cleanliness, lighting, heat, etc.) except this one. It is the boundary between stress and bliss, both for the animal and its owner. You can lead a horse to water but you cannot make it drink, as the saying goes. And if a snake does not wish to eat, you will have problems.

In this chapter, we will discuss the many aspects of feeding venomous snakes. Theoretically speaking, as long as the keeper takes the accepted steps, he or she should have no problems. Every minute detail, from time of day to the size of the meal, can have a remarkably defined effect on a snake's eating habits. Some of course will eat like rabid dogs and consume everything that moves (these are naturally the ideal captives). There are others, though, that will prove difficult, so hopefully by the end of this section you will have learned how to cope with both situations.

FOOD ITEMS

One of the nice things about keeping snakes is the fact that their diets are frequently highly

Lizards are a popular venomous snake food item, but they are somewhat difficult for the keeper to supply on a regular basis. Photo of *Telescopus semiannulatus* by H. Nicolay.

Mice and rats are the most often seen captive snake food, for both venomous and non-venomous species alike. They are inexpensive and breed in large numbers. Photo of *Atheris squamiger* by A. van den Nieuwenhuizen.

varied. This of course is good news for the keeper, who may not be able to acquire one item but then has a choice of others. Let's examine some of the more common dietary preferences.

Mice

Perhaps the most often seen element in the snake diet is the mouse. Larger snakes, generally speaking, are mammal-eaters.

Mice, as most of us know, are small, furry rodents that, among other characteristics, have a remarkable rate of reproduction. The gestation period for a healthy adult female is 21 days, which means they are a cinch to breed.

If you would like to take a shot at mouse breeding yourself, what you must first do is find a suitable location. This should of course have a generous degree of air circulation because mice can tend to smell. An isolated basement room with a window, or even a garage, will do fine.

Then, you must provide suitable housing. Since mice can generally be matched in quartets (one male and three females), your best bet is the use of a 10-

Mice and rats are commmonly available in many different sizes, which is good news for the hobbyist who has many different sized snakes. Photo of *Bitis nasicornis* by William B. Allen, Jr.

gallon aquarium or a similar cage. Perhaps a four to one ratio can even be used here, but any more than that and you run the risk of constant competition among the adults, and that of course leads to dead mice.

A more than adequate cage bedding for your mouse tank is wood shavings, but be careful not to use those of the cedar variety. Cedar contains oils which are toxic to snakes, venomous species not withstanding. Pine is better, probably the best in fact. Although it does not contain the odor-fighting qualities of cedar, it is certainly cheaper and a lot safer.

Mice, like other living things, require water. Provide them with a large bottle with a ball-tube tip on the dispenser. This will reduce the possibility of leakage, which wets the bedding and often causes many mice to attack and kill their young. Make sure the bottle is always at least half full; an empty bottle will also cause fatalities since mice who have nothing to drink seem to turn very violent. Be

When offering dead food, it is best to use forceps, for the obvious reasons. Photo of *Dothrops schlegeli* taking a pinkie by Jim Merli.

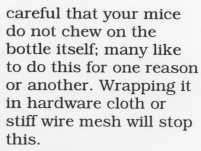

careful that your mice do not chew on the bottle itself; many like to do this for one reason or another. Wrapping it in hardware cloth or stiff wire mesh will stop this.

For food, mice are very keen on the pleasures of ordinary

believe that when the young are first born, the mother and her ensuing litter should be removed immediately. This is due to the belief that they (the young) will be summarily killed if left in the company of other adults. The reader may do this if he or she

After some time, many species will learn to accept dead food on a regular basis. Most keepers seem to favor dead food over live. Photo of *Bitis gabonica* by Jim Merli.

bird seed, which can be purchased in numerous places, mixed with a high-vitamin variety of dry dog food (kibble). The author bred mice for years on this simple, two-part diet and never had any problems with growth or breeding.

Some mouse breeders

wishes, but the author feels the newborns will be safe enough if the tanks are kept clean and the stock is well-fed. Simple separation of the male is no replacement for hygiene. Of course, you will always run the risk of losing a few young here and there, but the idea is to keep that to a minimum.

Which leads into the next topic, cage

be cleaned weekly without fail. The author did this on a constant basis and insists that it must be done faithfully

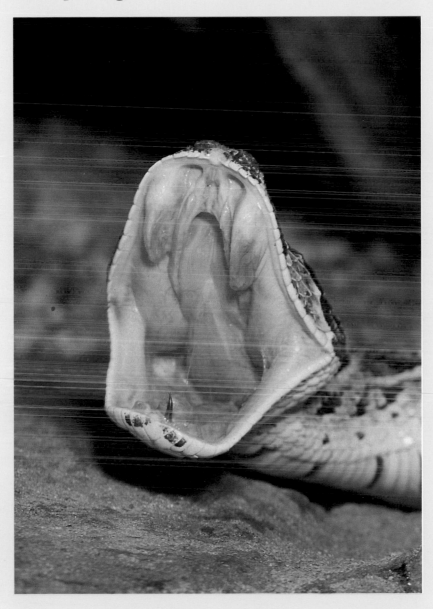

Notice how the fangs in this solenoglyphus Russell's Viper, *Vipera russelli*, are not yet fully extended, since it has not yet made contact with its prey. Photo by A, van den Nieuwenhuizen.

cleaning. Since hygiene in mouse breeding is so important for successful reproduction and rearing, all cages should

to achieve the desired results. Warm, soapy water with bleach, then rinsing with cold water, is perfectly fine. Do not wash the water bottles with bleach, however, as the residue is sometimes difficult to completely remove and can cause fatalities.

week or so after they've stopped nursing. The breeding females should be "renewed" with fresh stock about every six months, since they tend

In this photo the fangs have already struck the prey animal and the viper's left fang is beginning to "walk" over the food. Photo by A. van den Nieuwenhuizen.

As the mice grow, they can be removed and placed in their own "group tank" about a

to "burnout" after this time. This practice will give the breeder an unbroken flow of food.

One final note. If you are the type who finds the idea of mouse breeding, for whatever reason, not to your liking, you can obtain available in all sizes, and best of all, the headaches that can go along with breeding them are avoided completely.

Having secured a prey animal, venom will perform its secondary function and begin digesting the rat's tissues. Some believe this to in fact be a venom's primary function, and actual killing of the prey to be the second. Photo by A. van den Nieuwenhuizen.

mice easily enough through your local pet store. They are fairly inexpensive, should be Some keepers prefer to feed their venomous snakes mice that have either been pre-killed or thawed from freezing. The live-dead issue is certainly a hot one, even in the case of animals that are as capable of killing prey as venomous snakes. Therefore, the author has decided to walk the fence and leave such a decision solely up to the hobbyist. If you decide to train your snake to accept dead mice, you can purchase them frozen through either a pet store or one of the many mail-order dealers that seem to be appearing these days, or buy them live and kill them yourself. If you decide to do the latter, please execute the task in a reasonably humane way. There is no excuse for making the animal suffer any more than it has to. A good, strong mousetrap placed in a bucket with a top is advised.

Rats

Along the same line with mice are rats, though they are not completely the same. For one, they are much larger. This means that if you plan to breed them on your own you will have to provide more food, more shavings, and more space, not to mention that a bite from a rat is considerably more painful than one from a mouse.

Rats are perhaps best fed to snakes in a deceased state since they can inflict severe damage on a snake much faster than can a mouse. They have a completely different odor about them as well, so just because you have a snake that takes mice doesn't necessarily mean it will take rats too.

These can also be obtained at your local pet store with some regularity. But if you still wish to try breeding them, increase everything from mouse breeding about three times. A three to one quartet will need at least four square feet of ground space, and certainly triple the food and water. The young are born after a 23-day gestation period, one day longer than mice.

Frogs and Toads

Surprisingly enough, a large number of venomous snakes enjoy these as part of their diet. With highly aquatic

species like the water moccasin, *Agkistrodon piscivorus*, this comes as no surprise. Then again, there have also been reported cases of copperheads and certain adders going after frogs and/or toads as well. If these are available in your area, whether it be commercially or in the wild, they are certainly a good meal, but breeding them on the whole is a little too much trouble no matter what the situation. If they are not easily obtainable, then finding an alternative is advised. As usual, check all local laws before collecting amphibians.

Frogs and toads are not often bred in captivity as a food item. Photo of the Rhombic Night Adder, *Causus rhombeatus,* by A. van den Nieuwenhuizen.

Other Snakes

It seems rather unfortunate, and a bit hypocritical, that for the sake of thoroughness a small mention on the subject of snakes as a food source must be made. But the truth is, ophiophagy in venomous snakes is very common.

King Cobras, *Ophiophagus hannah*, for example, are classic snake-eaters. Many are sitting in zoos right now waiting for their next three or four Bullsnakes. Coral snakes (*Micrurus* species) are also snake-eaters. As keepers we should not be pleased with this, but there is not much to be done about it.

If you feel you would like to keep a snake-eating venomous serpent, you could do one of a few things for its nutritional health.

Firstly, you could submit yourself to the brutal experience of purchasing large-bodied ophidians on a weekly basis. This is of course fine for the captive, but a financial massacre of the highest order for the keeper, and probably a blow to the morale as well.

Secondly, you could try going out and finding snakes yourself. This however, even if wild-collecting is permitted in your area, is very irresponsible and can seriously damage your local environment.

Thirdly, and possibly the most reasonable option, is to actually establish a colony of

large, common snakes like racers, coachwhips, etc. and then go to the trouble of raising them up to adult size. Some species may not be terribly easy to breed, but it has been done.

Finally, you could attempt to sidestep the problem completely and try to wean your snake onto something else. Of course, this almost always requires constant contact with the animal and is consequently a dependable way to get yourself seriously injured.

As you can see, keeping ophiophagus serpents is somewhat nonsensical to begin with. Sadly, there are many attractive species that fall into this category. Although some options have been given here, all in all the author feels such snakes should be pretty much avoided.

Birds

Finally, many venomous snakes are keen on taking birds as a routine part of their diet. The Boomslang and the mambas jump to mind. It almost goes without saying that these particular species are almost exclusively arboreal (tree-dwelling), and thus have a familiarity with nests, etc.

Birds can be obtained a few ways, but the simplest and most advisable approach is by purchasing day-old chicks from a local supplier. Sometimes these can be obtained frozen. An interesting point which is worth noting here is that chicks which are only one day old are actually more nutritional for your snakes than those that are, say, even only two days older. This is because much of the yolk from the egg is still contained in the young chick's body, and thus will be passed on to the snake that takes it.

FORCE-FEEDING

Sometimes you might encounter a situation where force-feeding one of your snakes is warranted. As some readers may already know, this is difficult enough with non-venomous species. Therefore, it must be stressed first off that handling venomous snakes for any reason, even in matters of health, is very ill-advised and consequently to be discouraged. A task such as successfully force-feeding a venomous animal should be left strictly to an experienced professional or a trained veterinarian, thus the author does not feel it worth taking the risk of encouraging this dangerous activity.

TIME OF DAY/WEEK

Generally speaking, most snakes, whether they are venomous or not, prefer to eat in private. Thus, many will only eat at the times they would in the wild. Some are nocturnal and

Force-feeding venomous snakes requires an enormous degree of concentration. Clockwise from upper left: Sliding in the bar; turning it sideways; flipping it up to open the mouth; and finally, after the food has been slipped into the gullet, gently massaging the throat to encourage the food downward. Photos of *Boiga dendrophila* by S. Kochetov.

Since snakes are attracted to fish mostly by their smell rather than their movement, dead fish are usually taken as often as live ones. Photo of *Homalopsis buccata* by A. van den Nieuwenhuizen.

others are diurnal. If you can find out this information about the species you have, all the better. Correlate that with what time of day you feed it. Then, estimate how often it will feed by judging from its size and approximate age. The young of almost all snakes will eat more often than will the adults, so if possible, give them a normal-sized meal about twice per week. As they grow older, this will turn to about every four days, then five, and then finally, about once every week will be fine, perhaps every fortnight if the meal is considerable enough.

MEAL SIZES

Some venomous snakes love to eat. Many will just mechanically keep grabbing and eating as long as food is set in front of them.

This is not good. A snake of any kind should not have a belly that is too full, because

To have a snake take a prey animal by the head is usually more preferable than by the tail. Photo by A. van den Nieuwenhuizen.

this can cause a multitude of problems. A good rule to follow is to avoid creating lumps in the stomach that can be easily spotted by the naked eye from more than 15 feet away. Use your own judgment as to what exactly is "too much." The meals should be moderate and properly sized. If a snake has too much trouble getting something through the mouth, chances are it is too big.

REFUSAL TO EAT

If you have a venomous snake that does not seem to want to eat, you must first ask yourself the question, "Is

As you can see here, a snake can indeed swallow a prey item much larger than the size of its head. Photo by A. van den Nieuwonhuizen.

it losing any weight or does it seem otherwise in poor health?" If the answer is no, then the general rule of thumb to follow is, just leave it alone. Many venomous snakes go through a period of what is called "estivation" in which their bodies take a "rest" of sorts, and simply live off fats stored up from when they were last eating regularly.

However, if you suspect something else, you can either try a variety of "tricks" (covering the cage, raising or lowering heat, humidity, photoperiods, etc., trying live or dead foods, trying different

After taking a meal, a snake should be left alone for at least three days to allow digestion. Otherwise, a food item could very easily be regurgitated. Photo by A. van den Nieuwenhuizen.

foods, etc.) or simply try to discern whether or not the snake has a health problem that needs medical attention. If the latter is the case, the animal in question should be brought to a professional veterinarian.

REPRODUCTION AND CAPTIVE BREEDING

Facing page: A pair of Wagler's Pit Vipers, *Trimeresurus wagleri*. These are currently very popular in the herp hobby. Photo by A. van den Nieuwenhuizen.

There is a word in today's modern herpetological hobby, one that was spotlighted in the preface of this book, known as "herpetoculturing." For the benefit of new hobbyists, this is a modern term for captive breeding. As most serious hobbyists who keep non-venomous species are already aware, breeding some snakes is not all that difficult. A few, in fact, could readily be termed "easy."

But can this apply to any species of venomous snakes as well? Are there in fact a lot of major differences in the domestic procreation of poisonous serpents as opposed to those that aren't? This is the topic we will be dealing with in this chapter.

One final point. Since there are obviously many species to be dealt with under such a broad topic, instead of trying to tackle the monumental task of covering them all individually, the subject of captive reproduction will be offered in a general, more abstract fashion, giving specific hints toward different "types" of breeders (subtropical species, desert-dwellers, etc.) Through further study on the reader's part, he or she can then fit their own particular animals into one of the categories outlined.

PREPARATIONS

If you have decided to take a shot at breeding venomous snakes, there are a few things that must be considered beforehand. Procreation of the species is most certainly not a "let's put them together and just see what happens" type of situation.

Health Considerations

Firstly, you must concern yourself with the question "Are my snakes healthy?" Start off with something simple: weight. Do they look well-nourished? A skinny, underfed female is not going to produce well, if she even produces at all. One rule

Health is undoubtedly one of the most important considerations when attempting to captive breed any snakes. Notice how clear and unblemished the scales are on this *Leptodeira septentrionalis*, particularly around the ocular region. Photo by K. T. Nemuras.

of thumb to follow is to always make sure whichever two snakes you are going to breed are eating well and on schedule. Perhaps the most important reason for this is because you will have to hibernate, or at least "cool," them, and in order to do this, they must have enough fats stored in their tissues to survive while they are, shall we say, "resting."

Next, take steps to assure that the animals in question are not suffering from any diseases or ailments, as this too will obviously affect the breeding cycle. Any points of diminished health will be a loose cog in the reproductive machine. If you find that one of your specimens is suffering from something, be sure to have it cured before you hibernate it; many inexperienced keepers have made the mistake of thinking a quick period of enforced rest will "drive away" an offending problem. This

Girth is an important factor when identifying healthy snakes for breeding. Those snakes which look scrawny and undernourished will probably not reproduce. Photo of *Atheris squamiger* by Jim Merli.

is not so, and often such actions will worsen the problem rather than lessen it.

Another consideration is age of the parents relative to sexual maturity and relative to each other. You will have to do some research on your own to find out exactly when your particular species becomes sexually mature; and don't be fooled—this has virtually nothing to do with size. This is a rule best illustrated by a few of the breeders who might be called "unethical" and force their young to eat much more than they would naturally, figuring they will grow "large enough" to breed in half the normal time. In the long run this does not produce any more eggs or young, but it does create some very unhealthy snakes. It is a cruel practice, and one to which you as a conscientious keeper

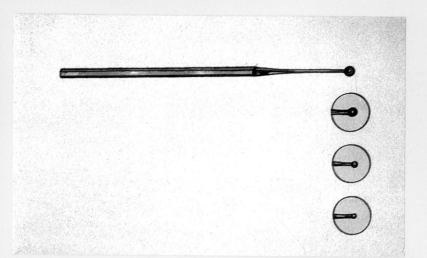

Detail of a sexing probe, with emphasis on the ball-shaped tips. Realistically speaking, three sizes are all you will probably ever need. Artwork by Larry Nelson.

should neither fall prey nor subscribe.

As for age of the parents relative to each other, unless the numbers have a vast space between them, there is no general cause for concern. It is of course best to have two snakes of similar sizes and ages, ideally speaking.

Sex Determination

A seemingly obvious consideration before breeding can be attempted, and yet one that many hobbyists are not adroit at, is the determination of males from females. Naturally it would be somewhat difficult to mate two snakes that were not of opposite sexes, and yet when it comes to those that are venomous, finding out the necessary answers is a tricky procedure.

With non-venomous species, the use of a long, thin, ball-tipped implement called a "probe" is most common. This is inserted into the cloaca on either side and slid posteriorly into a small "pocket" where either a scent gland (female) or a hemipene (male) is situated. If it moves in beyond three or four scales, chances are the animal is male. If it meets a barrier right away, it is female.

With a cobra or a rattlesnake, this kind of practice is going to be met with a good deal of animosity to say the least. It is best to let a trained professional handle such things in that situation, otherwise you run the risk of being struck.

There are a few other ways you can make an educated guess as to the gender of the snake you have. The most common is by judging from the width of the snake's body just where the "tail" begins, right after the vent. Generally speaking, it will not taper off as quickly in

most crucial natural process you must replicate in order to ensure successful reproduction. It really should be clarified right now that the reasoning behind the necessity for it is only abstract at best, because some species (those which occur in non-temperate

Species from tropical climes are not "hibernated" in the traditional sense, but instead go through a "wet/dry" season. Photo of *Trimeresurus purpureomaculatus* by W. Wuster.

males. With females, the inward curve of both sides much more abrupt.

Triggering the Sex Hormones (Hibernation and Wet/Dry Seasons)
    This is perhaps the

regions, especially tropical species) do not need to be "hibernated," in the typical sense. Hibernation, in essence, is the period of enforced rest that temperate-region snakes must endure for the efficient triggering of sex hormones. But with the warm-region species, this triggering is brought on by what is commonly referred to as the wet-dry seasons. For the purpose of this discussion, we will first cover aspects of the hibernation process relative to those species that come from temperate (colder) climates, and then give some general advice to those who wish to breed the others.

The first step in accurately simulating hibernation is to find out as much as you can about the natural hibernating conditions of the particular snakes you are planning to breed. This is extremely important, for some serpents only need a few weeks of hibernation, whereas others may need a few months. Where some will hibernate at very low temperatures, others need only mild surroundings.

A very successful method, used by breeders time and time again, is to simply find a cool corner of your home or wherever you are keeping your specimens and give them a soft substrate and a small bowl of water. Hook up a small heater with a thermostat control in the event that the temperature drops too low at any given time. Do not let their state of torpor fool you—they

A neonate (just born) example of the Timber Rattlesnake, *Crotalus horridus*. Photo by R. T. Zappalorti.

should still not be touched—but check the animals regularly to make sure they are alive and well and that the water bowl is at least one-third filled. Anywhere from one to three months should do it for most temperate species.

Now, for those snakes which are native to the warmer areas of the world, successfully replicating the changes they need in order to place them in breeding condition depends largely (almost entirely) on how these conditions occur in

their natural habitat. For the most part, the wet and dry seasons are simply that: a cycle which involves a period when the climate is dry and cool (which is when they "rest," although food will still be taken), and then a second period when the humidity and temperature rise greatly and the "rains" begin, thus signaling that it is time to breed.

When attempting to duplicate this cycle in captivity you must remember that the dry season does not require a massive drop in temperature in the same sense that it does in temperate regions. 62-65°F is most certainly cool enough, and any lower than that could kill many tropical species. As I said before, they can be fed during this time, but certainly not as much.

Then, after about three months, the temperature is gradually raised to anywhere from 80-88°F, and a virtually constant "misting" should be performed to recreate the rainy season. This tells the animals that their period of reduced activity is over and it is time to procreate.

THE BREEDING PROCESS

After removing the animals from their "resting" state (do this slowly, do not "shock" them out of it by placing them in a warm environment too soon), you should keep the males and the females separated. Give them about another two to three weeks to get going again, allowing them to shed. Begin feeding them as usual.

Then, place the female into the male's tank and just wait. Copulation may not commence right away, and when it does it can take anywhere from 15 minutes to a couple of hours to finish. Keep in mind that many venomous snakes (again, you have to know something about the species in question) only breed every other year in the wild, so don't be surprised if one year your pair ignore each other completely and then do the opposite the next.

After successful mating, you can try the pair again over the course of the next three

Facing page: Note the bright yellow tail on this Cantil, *Agkistrodon bilineatus taylori*. The young of the *Agkistrodon* use this trait to attract prey. Photo by M. J. Cox.

Using damp sphagnum moss in a plastic shoebox is an excellent way to incubate snake eggs. Shown are the eggs of the Cape Coral Snake, *Aspidelaps lubricus*. Photo by Jim Merli.

weeks to ensure fertility of the female (providing, of course, the male is not sterile). Then, be sure to provide her with exactly whatever requirements she needs. Temperature, cleanliness, and privacy are all major concerns when taking care of a pregnant snake. Stress can easily cancel out the chances of a good brood, so keep your husbandry skills sharp. If the mother is oviparous (egglaying), make sure she is given a box with some moist vermiculite. If she is viviparous (live-bearing) make sure she has a dark, quiet spot in which to give birth.

Concerning eggs, the

vermiculite mentioned above is, in the author's opinion, the most reliable method of egg incubation. A clear plastic shoebox with about a 1.5-inch layer of thick, granular, moistened vermiculite is very dependable. This can be purchased through almost any

Above: When using any type of incubating medium, it is generally not a good idea to cover the eggs completely. Photo by Jim Merli.

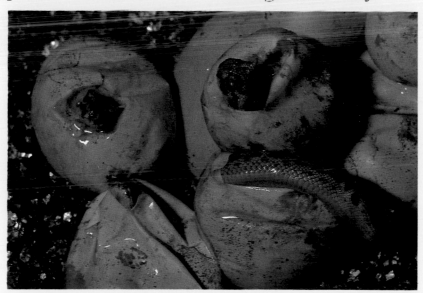

Left: Hatchling Desert Horned Vipers, *Cerastes cerastes*. Even at this age a venomous snake can be considered dangerous. Photo by K. H. Switak.

Above and Facing page: The fascinating birth of a Copperhead, *Agkistrodon contortrix*. Notice the opaque membrane in which the neonate is wrapped. The snake will break through this almost immediately. All photos by R. T. Zappalorti.

garden store. Keep the eggs warm and do not turn them; they should be placed exactly in the position in which they were laid, This is very important because a rotated egg will cause the yolk to drop on top of the developing embryo, thus smothering and killing it.

When the young begin to hatch, you may see a small yolk sac still attached. Many keepers feel this should be removed immediately; it should not. Let the animal go through the yolk absortion process on its own. The same applies to the umbilical cord of a live-born snake—nature will take care of it. Remember, a newborn venomous snake is almost always just as dangerous as its parents (in proportion to size, of course).

Finally, sometimes newborn snakes are unwilling feeders, and you may have trouble

As neonates, many snakes, like this Cape Coral Snake, *Aspidelaps lubricus*, resemble their parents almost exactly. Photo by Jim Merli.

getting them started. The key here is to have patience. If you find you cannot get them eating on their own even after you have tried a wide variety of known items, you will then have to make the decision to either release them into the wild (provided of course you have access to their natural habitat), pass them on to a more experienced herpetologist or a zoo, or allow a vet to try force-feeding. Never try the latter on your own.

SICKNESS AND DISEASE

In any type of book that deals exclusively with the life of a particular animal or group of animals, whether it be for the hobbyist, the student, or the general public, it is always a good idea to have a discussion on the subject of sickness and disease. If nothing else, the reader will then be exposed to the microtopics that lie therein, and perhaps even find genuine, practical uses for such information in the future.

But let me preface the pages that follow by saying that many of the ailments discussed may seem somewhat familiar to those of you who are already familiar with the world of non-venomous species. This is mainly because, on the topic of health and any lack of it, there is very little distinction between venomous and non-venomous snakes in the first place. Let me also

Notice the ugly wound on the dorsum of this viper and the cream that is being applied. Such work on venomous snakes can be very dangerous and should only be undertaken by professionals. Photo by S. Kochetov.

Keeping your snakes as healthy as this Pug-nosed Pit Viper, *Trimeresurus puniceus*, is the best way to treat disease: by avoiding it in the first place. Photo by W. Wuster.

say, and perhaps most importantly stress, that just because a section on venomous snake ailments has been included, this in no way means the author wishes the reader to attempt any at-home veterinary practices. Indeed, if you find that a venomous snake of yours has become ill and is even under the threat of losing its life, it should not be treated in any way by anyone other than a qualified professional.

Having said all that, I can now move forward more comfortably into this chapter and onto what is the first, and probably most sensible, aspect of venomous snake disease: avoiding it in the first place.

PREVENTIVE MEDICINE

As you already know, unless you are a vet you should never touch a venomous snake; but does this mean there is nothing you can do to maintain its health? Of course not. In fact, you are the single most important factor in a snake's health in the first place. It is not a matter of treating an animal once it has become sick, but avoiding that sickness to begin with. Remember the golden rule of herpetological husbandry: once a reptile or amphibian is eating on its own, the rest is purely up to the keeper.

The keys to preventive measures, at least within the keeper's power, are time, patience, and attention. These are the three main features of good husbandry, and that in turn becomes a synonym for effective preventive medicine.

Firstly, cleanliness.

As a competent hobbyist, you should set a reasonable cleaning schedule for yourself and stick to it. There is a short section elsewhere in this book outlining a cleaning technique that can be relied upon safely.

Next, set another schedule, this one for feeding, and stick to this as well. Of course, much of the efficiency involved in this scenario is dependent on the snake's willingness to eat to begin with, but if it is a hungry, eager type, then there is no excuse

Preventive medicine is really nothing more than giving strict attention to husbandry detail. Photo of Pope's Tree Viper, *Trimeresurus popeorum*, by W. Wuster.

for its going unfed.

Finally, make every effort to keep your snake's stress level as low as possible. As more people are beginning to realize, stress is not something suffered purely by humans. Since reptiles and amphibians are generally not good captives, they are a bit more susceptible to stress than, say, some of the more domestic animals like dogs or cats. Loud noises, a multitude of people, improper surroundings—all of these things and many others cause stress. A stressed snake shows signs of strain through abrupt fasts, increased irritability, etc. Look for the clues, and react.

DISEASES

Now we will discuss some of the more common illnesses your venomous snakes may fall victim to during their tenure in captivity. As the author mentioned earlier, possible cures will not be suggested (at least where actual physical contact is involved), for the obvious reasons.

The "Fer-de-Lance" Virus

Description: Viral infection that attacks the respiratory system in many *Bothrops* species, almost always with a fatal conclusion. Highly contagious, the infection acquired from some form of contact with other infected snakes. Mainly contracted through either the air or dirty waterbowls. Further tests have concluded that it is also carried in some *Elaphe*, *Dendroapsis*, and *Spilotes* species, suggesting that it can possibly affect all snakes under the right circumstances. It was first described in Switzerland in 1976. The researchers reported the original virus coming from a Western Diamondback Rattlesnake, *Crotalus atrox*. It is a paramyxovirus (PMV).

Symptoms: Clinical signs usually last from 5-12 days and consist of four major stages. During Stage 1, the snake displays a loss of muscle tone and appears stretched out in a linear posture with the head elevated slightly. Then in Stage 2, the snake will move about

restlessly with its mouth partially open. The tongue is not completely withdrawn, and the pupils will begin to dilate. In Stage 3, which is no more than a day from the victim's death, the mouth is kept opened even wider and a purulent material (pus) is expelled from the glottis. Finally, during Stage 4 (which lasts from only minutes to one hour before death), the mouth is wide open, the animal is very active, and the pupils are dilated.

Action: If you suspect this disease to have invaded a certain member of your collection, quarantine the snake in question and contact a veterinarian for further advice. At the time of writing, there is still no known effective treatment.

Respiratory/Lung Infection
Description: A bacterial infection that attacks the lungs, usually initiated by cold drafts, chills, etc., promoted by improper attention to temperature on the part of the keeper. Stress is also a large factor in the development of this affliction.

The Fer-de-Lance, *Bothrops atrox*, is one of the many *Bothrops* species which can be affected by the virus named after it. Photo by R. T. Zappalorti.

The Fer-de-Lance Virus was first described in 1976 in Switzerland and is known to mostly affect *Bothrops* vipers. It is highly contagious and has wiped out entire collections in less than a fortnight. Photo of *Bothrops lateralis* by B. Kahl.

Symptoms: Occasional wheezing, mucous discharge from the mouth and nose, and a sudden refusal to eat.

Action: Increase temperature to required level, terminate all draft-causing agents (i.e., open windows, doors, etc.), and contact a veterinarian.

and further into the digestive tract. Very dangerous in its later stages and should be dealt with immediately.

Symptoms: The snake will move about with its mouth slightly open, and a visible softening of the gums will appear. The infected area will be white and sometimes

Mouth rot can cause a snake great pain and suffering if it is allowed to develop to this point. (Notice also the double fangs.) Photo by William B. Allen, Jr.

Mouth Rot/Infectious Stomatitis

Description: A bacterial infection leading to a severe lack of vitamins A and C, that softens up the tissues in and around the jaw, thus loosening the animal's teeth, causing feeding to be very painful. Can spread down into the throat

cheesy due to swelling of the surrounding membranes.

Action: Keep patient in a warm, very clean cage and consult a vet.

Salmonella

Description: Another bacterial infection, this one invading the digestive tract. Can spread to other cagemates, cause occasional deaths, and even infect humans (through contact with soiled cage apparatus).

Symptoms: Hard to tell. Many captive reptiles carry the salmonella bacteria in one form or another. In extreme cases, extraordinary feces (off-colored or in diarrhea form) will be discharged.

Action: Mostly preventive, in the form of good hygiene practices. If you suspect an infected specimen, quarantine it and call your vet.

Mites/Ticks

Description: Tiny parasites that mostly invade the body surface. Mites appear as tiny, dark dots moving about mainly at night. Ticks are somewhat larger and latch on to the animal in order to suck blood. They both frequently carry a number of diseases with them, thus infecting the host as well.

Symptoms: With mites, venomous snakes and non-venomous as well frequently lose their appetite and spend an inordinate amount of time in their water containers. They sometimes rub up against cage objects in order to relieve the irritation.

With ticks, the infestation often only consists of one or two invaders, these appearing as small "blisters" protruding from under the scales and growing larger as they fill with the

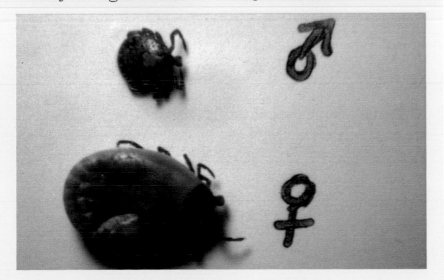

Ticks and mites are perhaps the most common ectoparasites found on snakes. Photo of male and female tick by Dr. Fredric L. Frye, in *Reptile Care*.

Sometimes endoparasitic infestations can become so severe that they will be clearly visible in the oral cavity, like the flukes shown here. Photo by Dr. Fredric L. Frye, in *Reptile Care*.

animal's blood. If they have dug deep enough into the snake, it may lose its desire for food and may become slightly irritable.

Action: Since so many complications can arise, mites and ticks should be dealt with as soon as possible. The former can be treated to a certain extent by the keeper by placing a small (about 2 in by 2 in) piece of pest strip (small, rectangular bars of plastic impregnated with pesticides that people hang from screened porches, etc. to kill flying insects, etc.) in a container with a series of holes drilled in the container top. This is then placed (with tongs—and even then, very carefully) into the tank for about four days. Repeat the treatment in a week to kill of any newly hatched young.

The ticks, however, require much greater contact and must therefore be removed by way of tweezers by a trained professional.

One further note. Once either of these problems has been alleviated, the tank, all its apparatus, and the immediate area surrounding the tank should be thoroughly washed and rinsed. Wood products should be burned and replaced (since mites often crawl inside deep cracks in wood).

Tapeworms

Description: An infestation of a type of parasitic flatworm usually attacking the digestive system, sometimes going so far as to being externally visible (just below the skin surface) in the secondary larval stages of certain species.

Symptoms: These worms usually can be detected early on in fecal samples, but if further developed, the patient will lose its appetite and show signs of severe lethargy.

Action: If this ailment is suspected, very carefully remove fecal samples and have a

Tapeworms are common endoparasites that usually attack the digestive system. A hobbyist should have a snake's feces checked for tapeworm eggs at least twice a year. Photo by William B. Allen, Jr.

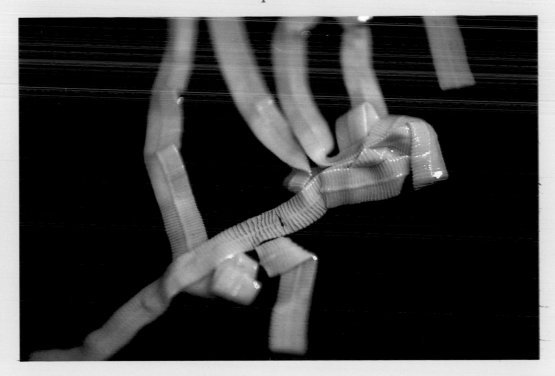

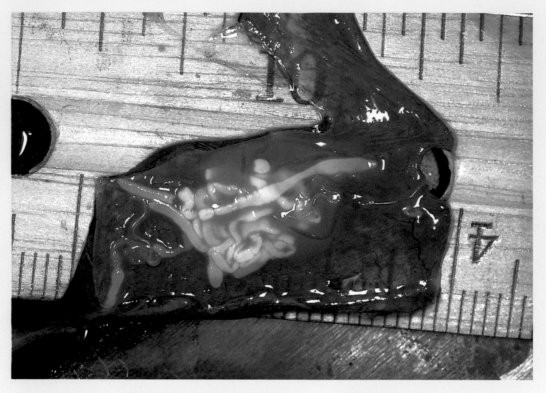

Tapeworms can grow to a fairly respectable size and may cause much damage if undetected. Photo by Paul Freed.

veterinarian examine them. Chances are, he or she will then advise you to bring the animal in for anthelminthic treatment. Many keepers routinely have feces checked for worm eggs several times a year.

Roundworms

Description: Similar to tapeworms, these worms usually infest the digestive tract. They can cause severe tissue damage in extreme cases.

Symptoms: Patient loses its appetite and becomes lethargic. Feces may appear off-colored.

Action: At one time it was believed that an effective at-home treatment involved placing a large bowl of warm (85°F-90°F) water into the patient's tank and coaxing it to bathe. This supposedly helped "flush out" many of the offending organisms, but in time it was learned that this "treatment" did not in fact produce any positive results at all. The most sensible thing a keeper can do is to present a fecal sample to a professional for examination.

Infections of the Eye

Description: Cuts, abrasions, swellings, etc. in and around the ocular region, all of which are susceptible to bacterial infection.

Symptoms: Visible swellings or other unusual physical qualities of the eyes and their surrounding scales.

Action: Consult a veterinarian. All eye work is extremely delicate and requires much physical contact with the patient.

Skin Infections (blisters, abscesses, etc.)

Description: Any unusual imperfections on the skin surface of the animal. Common in water and garter snakes, etc. as these animals frequent water more often than other species.

Symptoms: Unless the condition is extreme, the patient does not seem overtly affected by these problems.

Action: Since many types of treatments must be administered through direct physical contact with the animal, it is best to seek professional help. However, keeping an animal's tank in tune with its natural environment as much as possible is one way of

Difficulty with shedding (dysecdysis) is a very common problem with captive snakes, but dealing with this in venomous species is a very delicate, very dangerous affair. Photo of an *Agkistrodon* sp. by S. Kochetov.

avoiding many skin infections to begin with.

Severe Cuts and Lacerations

Description: Openings on the snake's skin surface, usually caused by fights with cagemates, violent food animals, or even sharp objects that have somehow found their way into the tank (i.e.,

Maintaining proper humidity is one of the key elements to consistently successful ecdysis. When a snake's skin gets too dry, it is not able to peel off smoothly. Photo by Ron Everhart of Timber Rattlesnake, *Crotalus horridus*, during a good shed.

cages breaking, bulbs being smashed, etc.).

Symptoms: Severe bleeding, visible openings in the skin, and abnormal behavioral reactions by the animal.

Action: Since virtually all cuts, whether they be minor or major, are highly vulnerable to infection, they should be dealt with as soon as possible. With some of the calmer species, it is possible to dab smaller cuts with hydrogen peroxide on a cotton swab or something similar which has been fastened (taped) onto the end of a long stick. With larger cuts (lacerations), peroxide is useful as a first step treatment, but ultimately will not be sufficient and the patient will have to be brought to a professional. Never attempt to bandage a venomous snake.

Burns

Description: Swollen or inflamed lesions on the skin surface, sometimes bubbling or blistering (or actual sloughing of skin tissues in severe cases), usually as a result of too much contact with a hot rock, heat lamp, etc.

Symptoms: Visible marks on affected areas. Snake may spend long hours seeking relief in waterbowl and will very probably become irritable, although loss of appetite does not always occur.

Action: Some burn cream applied with a cotton swab fastened to a very long stick is helpful where some of the calmer species are concerned (and with milder burns), but otherwise a professional should be consulted; the more severe the burn, the faster it needs attention. Most burns

A wound is undoubtedly one of the most stressful problems a snake can endure. If it is deep, sutures will usually have to be applied. Photo by William B. Allen, Jr.

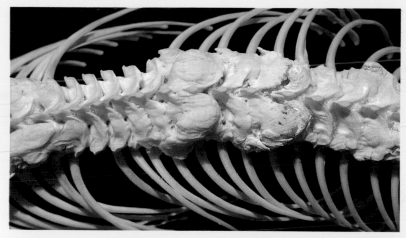

A snake's skeleton is more delicate than many people imagine and is highly susceptible to breakage. Photo by Dr. Fredric L. Frye, in *Reptile Care.*

are very susceptible to infection.

Broken Bones
   Description: Actual fracturing of the bone structure.
   Symptoms: Patient will not move much due to extreme pain. Definite loss of appetite; do not attempt to feed if you suspect this problem! Depending on the severity of the fracture, one or the other end of the broken bones may visibly push on the skin from the inside of the patient. In extreme cases, a puncturing through the surface may occur, thus leaving the patient vulnerable to a multitude of further complications, many of these leading to almost guaranteed fatality.
   Action: Patient must be moved as slowly and carefully as possible, and treated only by a professional. Sometimes the victim may have to

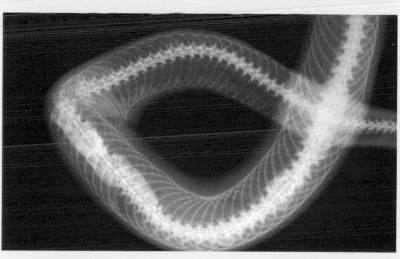

Note the severity of the break in this X-ray. It is realistic to assume that a snake suffering from a break of this kind will have much difficulty recovering completely. Photo by Dr. Fredric L. Frye, in *Reptile Care.*

be euthanized in the interests of humaneness.

Gout

Description: A general weakening and stiffening of a snake's internal organs, usually associated with joints, vertebrae, etc.

Symptoms: An extensive lethargy. Movements seem painful and difficult. Constipation is sometimes present. Loss of appetite is also concurrent.

Action: To comfort the inflicted animal, give it an increased degree of privacy along with a slight rise in humidity. Supply it with a bowlful of fresh, cool water and consult a veterinarian.

Hypervitaminosis

Description: This is a condition contracted by snakes that have simply received an overabundance of vitamins. It is an illness that affects quite a number of captive reptiles since many keepers are unaware that their pets can actually be given "too much" of a good thing.

Symptoms: Many, but mostly internal. Some external signs, like inexplicable swelling, may occasionally be present. Very difficult to detect.

Action: Simply cut back on vitamin supplementation. Determine a fair, responsible amount and give conservatively.

ANECDOTES

The author is honored to be able to treat the reader to a series of tales that have been provided by five of the most highly respected members of the herpetological community (and a sixth by the author himself). These can be used as sources of future reference, education, or just for the sake of reading pleasure.

JOSEPH T. COLLINS
(Herpetologist at the University of Kansas, and co-author of *A Field Guide to Reptiles and Amphibians, Eastern and Central North America*):

"I suffered a nasty bite from a Cottonmouth that was in a particularly vicious mood one day. The animal was seated in its tank, on the far left side, waiting. I put my hand in to retrieve its waterbowl, which was on the opposite side, and it nailed me.

"When I went to the hospital, the people who were working on me didn't bother checking to

The Cottonmouths, *Agkistrodon piscivorus*, are known for causing severe swelling and extensive tissue damage to bite victims, and in some cases even death. Photo by R. T. Zapplorti.

see if I was allergic to the antivenom, and consequently I had more of a reaction to that than the bite. I bloated up so much my feet squished when I walked. It took me weeks to get over that.

"And then I know of another Cottonmouth story, this one told to me by my good friend Mike Pearce, about a friend of his down in Arkansas.

"Jim is out with two pals on a boat one night on a swampy backwater, and a Cottonmouth falls in. Jim is in the middle of the craft and the snake lands right at his feet. When he jumps back, his leg catches the cable that leads from the battery to the only light.

"Suddenly it's three men alone on a swamp in the dark with a Cottonmouth, whereabouts unknown.

"Jim hears a splash. And then, in a little bit, another splash. So he jumps too. Now it's three men in the swamp and the snake in the boat. They tread water for several minutes, and then Jim hears this voice in the darkness.

" 'Jim? How many Cottonmouths did you

Cottonmouths are highly aquatic, living in swamps, marshes, etc., and although they are generally peaceful, they will not hesitate to bite a human aggressor. Photo by S. Kochetov.

say were in the boat?'

" 'One,' says Jim.

"Silence, then, 'Jim? How many do you reckon are out here?!'

"And finally, I remember a story told by one of my colleagues about a young assistant who was in Mexico trying to secure a rattler while on the edge of a cliff. Seems the snake bit him twice, then he fell backwards over the edge, and finally landed in a tree, one of the branches piercing his head. The amazing thing was, he not only sustained no permanent injury, but held on to the snake as well."

(Also appears in *The Topeka Capital-Journal*, August 9, 1992.)

DR. HOBART M. SMITH

(Professor of Herpetology at the University of Colorado, and the author of countless herpetological works for both hobbyists and scientists, including TFH's enormously popular *Snakes as Pets*):

"One of my luckiest known brushes with oblivion came one summer when I stayed a week or so at a very small ranch in the remote rainforests of Campeche, Mexico. It was a three-day trek from Ciudad del Carmen, up a large river by a commercial boat, up a small tributary by dugout, then across country by pack animal for another day. No other habitations existed for miles around. Night collecting was limited to a few trails, which I could walk by holding a lantern close in front of me so its light reflected from my clothing and my vision was protected from glare by the opaque top of the lantern. However, the gasoline I had brought with me was not well refined, and would clog the generator with carbon so badly that after a half or three-quarter hour I would have to scurry back to the ranch before the light gave out entirely. There I'd clean out the generator and start out again.

"The most common herp species were of the genus *Leptodeira*—two foot, slender, cross-barred snakes. These I would grab without precaution, for they could be handled with impunity despite their

The cat-eyed snakes, although rarely seen in captivity, are highly attractive serpents and seem generally harmelss in spite of the fact that they are opisthoglyphous. Photo of the Northern Cat-eyed Snake, *Leptodeira septentrionalis septentrionalis*, by Dr. Sherman A. Minton.

rear fangs. On one occasion, when my lantern had burned so dimly that I was at the point of returning again to clean it, another snake I assumed was a *Leptodeira* rapidly wiggled across the trail. As usual, I grabbed it near midbody and, since several species of *Leptodeira* occurred there, I set the lantern down and held the snake loosely in both hands close to the lantern to see better what species I had. To my vast astonishment, I was holding freely a Fer-de-Lance, *Bothrops asper*, perfectly capable of delivering a lethal bite at any time—and why it had not already done so I shall never know. Totally shocked, I dropped the snake instantly and then used something to pin its head down while I picked it up properly behind the head. I have frequently given fervent thanks that I was not bitten, for it would have been most arduous to obtain medical attention. I had with me no first aid equipment or antivenin, and did not then know how vital instantaneous incision and suction are to avoid the need for medical treatment.

"And then, judgment—poor, that is—came into play in the context of the first poisonous snakebite I ever received (I have been bitten

twice). When I was a freshman at Kansas State College in Manhattan, I spent a great deal of time (to the detriment of coursework, as I went on probation after that year) collecting snakes along Wildcat Creek west of town. I added them to the live herp exhibit maintained by Dr. Howard K. Gloyd on the top floor of the museum, where I acted as unpaid caretaker. On one trip I found an exceptionally large copperhead of which I was inordinately proud, for it was the largest I had ever seen. Late one afternoon while I was cleaning the cages, the janitor moseyed into the room, exchanging comments about the animals on exhibit and marvelling at anyone picking up the venomous ones. I assured him it was simple—one just pinned down the head and picked up the snake behind the head. Nonchalantly I offered to demonstrate how it was done, and hooked the big copperhead out of its cage and onto the smooth wooden floor. Pinning its head down with the wire hook, I reached down to pick up the snake behind the head when it jerked out from under the wire and in a flash bit the middle finger of my right hand. So much for the proper way to catch and hold a venomous snake.

"Although considerable swelling, pain, and nausea ensued, even after use of antivenin applied some 15 minutes later, no permanent injury was sustained—only an incredible caution in handling such animals, sufficient to carry through successfully the capture of hundreds since then."

The cat-eyed snakes, *Leptodeira,* are semi-arboreal, but spend most of their night hours on the ground hunting for frogs, lizards, etc. Photo by S. Kochetov.

Many professional workers who have had heavy interaction with the Saw-scaled Viper, *Echis carinatus*, consider it to be among the most dangerous snakes in the world. Photo by R. T. Zappalorti.

(Also appears in *Notes From Noah*, a publication of the Northern Ohio Association of Herpetologists, XI (4), 1984.)

DR. SHERMAN A. MINTON
(From the Indiana University School of Medicine, and author of multiple herpetological works, including the well-known *Venomous Reptiles*, co-authored with his wife, Madge):

"I have spent a considerable amount of time in the company of Saw-scaled Vipers, *Echis carinatus*, and there are two instances of singular behavior by these vipers that deserve description in detail. One snake was basking in a completely barren spot soon after sunrise. When alarmed, it came directly toward me, actually looping against my feet. I moved ten feet or so in a different direction, and

The Speckled Rattlesnake, *Crotalus mitchelli*, is an attractive although very nervous pit viper occurring primarily in the southwestern United States and some parts of Baja California. Photo by Ron Everhart.

the snake followed. By a series of such moves I led the reptile some 40 feet from the spot where I first saw it. Each time it stopped close to my feet, and often bit at them when I moved.

"In the second instance, the snake was routed out of cover in a euphorbia mound. It came directly toward me in a rapid sidewinding motion. When I sidestepped, it made for my daughter standing a few feet away. She also retreated, and the snake snapped into a defensive coil, striking at every moving object. It is easy to interpret such behavior as aggressive, but it is also possible that the snake was attracted by a shadow cast by a standing person. This might be seen by the frightened reptile as a shrub or rock offering possible refuge. Be that as it may, a barefoot person might easily be bitten under such circumstances. In this connection, one of my patients, bitten as he entered a bathhouse about dusk, said the snake 'chased him around the room until it was killed'."

(Also appears in the *Bull. Amer. Mus. Nat. Hist.*, 134, 1966.)

DR. ROGER CONANT

(Adjunct Professor of Biology at the University of New Mexico, and the author of such well-known herpetological works as the *Field Guide to Reptiles and Amphibians; Eastern and Central North America* in the Peterson series, the exhaustive work on the genus *Agkistrodon* and its allies, and the *Reptile Study* merit badge pamphlet for the Boy Scouts of America, not to mention more than 200 scientific papers and articles):

"My most vivid memory of an experience with a venomous snake was way back in 1929 when I was bitten on the left thumb by a speckled rattlesnake. I was only 20 years old at the time, and I had been taking photographs at the Toledo (Ohio) Zoo for a lecture I was planning.

"The doctor who was summoned made some disastrous mistakes. The old cut-and-suck method of first aid was then in vogue, but he slashed so deeply with his scalpel that he severed all the nerves and blood vessels and, in essence, amputated my thumb with that single stroke. Also, he failed to give me an anti-tetanus shot. Just 21 days later I came down with lockjaw, and I was one of the very few persons who ever survived that illness. After I had recovered,

A Northern Pacific Rattlesnake, *Crotalus viridis oreganus*, with a trio of newborns. Note the sharp contrast in coloration. Photo by Ron Everhart.

and the amputation had been done properly by a surgeon, the doctor left town. He could not face his peers.

DR. HENRY S. FITCH

(Author of the monumental *Autecology of the Copperhead*, plus a multitude of other works):

"Once when I was a graduate student doing field work for my garter snake dissertation (circa 1935), I had hunted along the Klamath River in Oregon and was driving south on a back road and saw a two-foot Pacific Rattlesnake cross in front of me. I caught the snake and tossed it into the bag of groceries I was carrying.

"A few miles farther on, at the California

Copperheads, *Agkistrodon contortrix*, are a much-studied group of solenoglyphs whose bites, interestingly enough, are rarely fatal to humans. Photo by Ron Everhart.

border, I was stopped at the state's fruit inspection station. The inspector questioned me as to where I had been and what fruits and vegetables I might be carrying. As we conversed he leaned through the open window of the rear door and began poking about through my load. I had forgotten about the snake and my main concern was that my well-hidden Oregon potatoes might be discovered. But then, for a hair-raising instant, I realized that the inspector had noticed the snake bag and was 'feeling up' the rattlesnake inside it. The snake remained passive, but evidently it did not have the feel of a citrus, and before I could catch my breath to remonstrate, the inspector had passed on to other parts of the load. Minutes later I was driving south into California, secure with my inspection certificate, but still a little weak in the knees. It is a mystery why the snake did not bite through the bag or even rattle, but that day I was lucky, and the inspector luckier than he knew.

"Then, in 1975, a high school biology class had come to the University of Kansas Natural History Reservation for a field trip and I took them on a short hike to show them my snake-trapping operation. In one trap I had a copperhead, which I removed, measured, weighed, and marked, while explaining procedures. As I was finishing, a student went to the trap 25 feet away at the other end of the drift fence and called to me, 'You got two!'. I explained that it was unusual to catch a snake at both ends of a drift fence; they were not all that common. I went to the second trap, opened it, dumped out the snake, held down the head with my stick, and picked it up, talking all the while. But still another copperhead was lying there. The two of them had been intertwined, and while I was holding down and grasping the first one, the second was free to bite me had it been so inclined. Much to my amazement, it did not.

An oddly colored Western Diamondback Rattlesnake, *Crotalus atrox*, with the traditional dusky tan base color much lighter than usual. Photo by S. Kochetov.

"And finally, June of 1992. As an octogenarian, I am handicapped by failing hearing and vision. I cannot hear rattlesnakes rattling, and miss much that I should be seeing in the field. One day as I turned a corrugated metal shelter, strategically placed to attract snakes, I exposed the rear end of a large copperhead just as it was sliding into a cottonrat burrow. I have striven to hone my reflexes for exigencies like this, and quick as a flash I grabbed the tail. But what I had not seen was that the snake was lying in a loop, mostly within the enlarged burrow entrance, facing outward, with its head only three to four inches from my fingers. It made a short lunge forward (not an actual strike). At that instant I saw its head and dropped it like a hot potato. Then I pinned it down and caught it, but ever since then I have tried to extend my safety margin with due allowance for faulty vision."

(From a personal letter to the author.)

W. P. MARA

"This story does not so much involve me, but a personal friend who has a strange affinity toward breeding poisonous snakes, including cobras, mambas, bamboo vipers, and rattlesnakes.

"It seems a friend of his had a Western Diamondback Rattlesnake, *Crotalus atrox*, that he claimed he had raised from a baby and which was indeed perfectly tame. In spite of my earlier doubts, I had to admit that I later found this to be somewhat accurate, as I did witness him on one occasion walking around with it on his neck, perfectly calm! He further stated that he would sit for hours watching television with it in his lap, and never once experienced any 'mishaps.' I did not venture a touch myself, as I was still convinced he was out of his mind and would one day most certainly 'get it.'

"Unfortunately, it was not he, but my breeder friend who became the victim. One afternoon the snake's owner brought his 'tame pet' over to the breeder's

house to show it off to a small crowd. After being placed in the breeder's lap, the snake promptly wiggled out and into one of the drawers of the desk he was sitting in front of. Sure that the snake would live up its reputation and remain sedate, the breeder grabbed the beast by the tail and tried pulling it back out. The snake then turned instantly and sank both fangs full-force into his right hand, in the soft, web-like area between the thumb and forefinger. My breeder friend eventually took a six-week stay at the local hospital, and is now unable to use three fingers—permanently.

"Finally, and very briefly, my grandfather, who died quite some years back, told me the tale of how his own grandfather was swimming in a small river in southern Florida and was suddenly bitten by a Cottonmouth at the base of the spine. Since he was not near a hospital (and since in those days there wasn't much that could be done anyway), my great-great grandfather suffered severe damage to his spinal cord and became crippled from the waist down for the remainder of his life."

The Western Diamondback Rattlesnake, *Crotalus atrox*, is widely bred in captivity, and as you can see here, an albino variety is also available. Photo by W. P. Mara.

VENOMOUS SNAKES AND MAN

Facing page:
Snake
charming has
been a
perpetual
source of
fascination
and intrigue
for centuries.
The snake
charmer
shown in this
photo is
performing in
Singapore
with a *Naja
naja*. Photo
by K. H.
Switak.

Man has had much interaction with venomous snakes through the centuries, and through this sometimes unpleasant relationship many interesting subjects have arisen. In the following paragraphs a few of them will be investigated.

Perhaps a good place to start would be with rattlesnake roundups. I say this because rattlesnake roundups seem to be a pretty "hot" issue at the moment. In this day and age of so many "ecologically minded" individuals, activities such as this seem to be on the wane and the conservation attitude on the ascent.

If we were to trace some history, we could safely assume that rattlesnake roundups began in the United States as far back as the late 1600's. Of course, back then it was not considered quite as much a "sport" as it is today, and the reasoning behind such actions was a little more understandable.

Early colonists did not have the knowledge of venomous snakes that we have today. In their eyes, a snake was a snake, they all presented danger, and thus should be killed on sight, especially those that had already caused human injuries before. Most roundups in those days were done for the purpose of clearing and securing areas for possible settlement. Whether the meat of venomous snakes was used for consumption the author does not know.

Through the years, however, the meaning of the rattlesnake roundup has changed drastically. These days it seems like nothing more than an exercise in machismo. Most contemporary roundups take place in the southern and western United States, the majority in Texas and Oklahoma (and some in Pennsylvania) where there are actual clubs

(usually some sort of social fraternity in conjunction with the township itself, which does much for civic publicity) that meet annually for the "main event." During such times, as many 500–1000 specimens can be taken. Oddly enough, these populations do not seem to suffer as dramatically as one might think, but many have still suffered enough in some places to where rattler roundups have been banned.

Often the people involved claim to be doing a "public service" by removing these "incredibly dangerous" animals, but in fact virtually all venomous snakes worldwide would rather avoid man than confront him. A rattlesnake only bites as a last resort, and certainly does not seek out human victims; the victims must go to it. The truth of the matter is, the participants are only putting themselves at risk, and there have certainly been more than a few injuries recorded, and even a number of deaths.

The techniques involved are rather simple: the roundups usually occur in early spring when the animals are just emerging from their dens, or even in late winter, when they can be trapped in dens

If and when this rattlesnake cast is correctly painted, it will be a beautiful piece of herpetological artwork. This is one way many hobbyists can enjoy the visual appeal of a venomous snake without having to own a live one. Photo by W. P. Mara.

in large, congested numbers. A trickle of gasoline is run down into the entranceway, thus flushing out the occupants. Catching them during the colder times is also easier because they will still be in a lethargic state and thus much more sluggish. I would also like to mention a further technique known as "snapping." With this, the "catcher" grabs the snake by its tail and literally "snaps" it, thus, assumedly, breaking its neck. Of course, especially in the case of some of the larger rattlers, this probably doesn't accomplish much more than irritating the snake to the point of actual rage; and that of course can lead to a bite.

After capture the snakes are then systematically brought to a central location where the curious can experience a "rattlesnake barbecue," watch specimens get milked, or even see their heads get chopped off and their bodies skinned, to be made into a variety of novelty items including key chains, boots, hats, wallets, belt buckles, boloties, and of course many other

As long as herp-oriented clothing is not made from the skins of the animals themselves, there is absolutely no harm in an item as attractive as this rattlesnake belt buckle. Photo by W. P. Mara.

bizarre things. The meat too has become quite a delicacy, and a handful of companies actually put it in cans and sell it on the mass market. The author must confess that he has tried it on one occasion (I was much younger and consequently unaware that I would be writing this book one day), and cannot honestly say the

Imprinted leather wallets are another of the many pieces that have surfaced from the snake-themed item craze. Photo by W. P. Mara.

taste was unpleasant. A little salty, but not disagreeable.

For the most part, rattlesnake roundups seem to be getting a little too sensational and are best ignored by the self-respecting hobbyist. At this time they don't seem to hold any truly beneficial effects for either man or the snakes (save for the occasional venom extraction).

Another interesting aspect of venomous snake sensationalism is their usage in religious ceremonies. Many radical sects in North America (most notably in an unmapped area known as the "Bible Belt") will take a venomous snake and, in order to prove their faith, will handle it freely. If you are interested in the history of this practice, Dr. Sherman Minton and his wife Madge say in their *Venomous Reptiles* that it all began in Grasshopper Valley, Tennessee, in 1908 with a farmer named George Hensley. Apparently what Mr. Hensley did was take a quote from the Bible (Mark 16:17 & 18) a bit literally. Without quoting directly, the two paragraphs stated that he who believes will be able to handle even the deadliest of animals and remain unharmed. True to his beliefs, Hensley then found himself a large rattler and did just that. Having been successful, he then brought it to his local church where he did it again, and again had success.

By the mid-1930's the practice had spread into Kentucky, and through

a single news article in 1938, it had "gone national." (Mr. Hensley, however, died in 1955 from—amazingly enough—a bite from an Eastern Diamondback Rattlesnake, *Crotalus adamanteus*, while performing a service.) Most recently, a 34-year-old man in Indiana was bitten on the hand while trying to remove a Timber Rattlesnake, *Crotalus horridus*, from a box during a ceremony for the "Hi-Way Holiness Church of God." According to the article, the practice is apparently not illegal (yet) unless the snake was obtained through illegal means or was an endangered species.

Elsewhere in the world, many venomous snakes are considered symbols of high regard and worship. There are so many cults that this can be applied to, it is futile to even attempt going over it. The King Cobra, *Ophiophagus*

Some belt buckles are extremely ornate and could literally be considered pieces of artwork in their own right. Photo by W. P. Mara.

hannah, for example, is highly feared in its native land, as are the mambas, *Dendroaspis*, the Boomslang, *Dispholidus typus*, and the Saw-scaled Viper, *Echis carinatus*.

In some countries women regard the cobra as a sign of fertility, and many will leave offerings at tunnel entrances in the hopes that by pleasing them they will increase their chances of becoming pregnant.

In certain parts of Malaya and Indonesia, Wagler's Pit Viper is considered a sign of good luck and is encouraged to live near domestic dwellings. Since it is a reasonably relaxed snake, many natives handle specimens freely, even feeding them by hand. There are of course the occasional reported bites, but rarely do any of them prove fatal.

A lot of primitive tribes used the dried venoms of many animals, including snakes, to prepare the tips of weapons. Darts, arrows, spears, were all coated with the various poisons of both plants and animals. On some occasions, the snake's heads were simply removed, spread open, and then connected to the projectile tips. An interesting sight to be sure!

And finally, perhaps the most memorable case of a venomous snake interacting with man (or in this case woman) is the famed death of the Queen of the Nile, Cleopatra. According to legend, she committed suicide by encouraging and then receiving the deadly bite. Many experts believe the agent to be an Egyptian Cobra or some type of an asp, which makes a fair amount of sense.

A FEW INTERESTING SPECIES

In any book such as this, it would seem almost foolish to spend a great deal of time and text talking about a certain type of animal without somewhere along the way offering examples of a few intriguing members of that particular group.

The choices I have made for this chapter are based on species that I have judged "interesting" from a general perspective and at which I thought they could best illustrate and represent similar species. They are arranged in alphabetical order according to genus.

NORTHERN COPPERHEAD
Agkistrodon contortrix mokasen

A member of one of the most commonly seen "pet" venomous snake genera, the Northern Copperhead has a lot going for it and its commercial popularity is certainly no surprise.

A depiction of the combat ritual that male copperheads perform at mating time. Artwork by Scott Boldt.

For one, it is a remarkably attractive animal. There is a series of beautiful dark brown "hourglass" saddles most prominent on the lateral region, with a lighter brown, or sometimes tan, interior. The base color is also a light, dusty brown, but can also appear gold or even light chocolate. The head boasts the traditional "arrowhead" shape and is usually true to the base color, with a slight darkening on the rostral scale, a thin dark stripe running through the eye, and labials that are slightly lighter.

The Northern Copperhead usually mates once every other year (bi-annually), and will produce a litter of anywhere from 8-10 young. These young will measure just under a foot in length and have notably bright yellow tails which are vibrated in leaf litter in order to attract prey. They are fairly easy to breed in captivity if the keeper does not mind waiting an extra year for the results.

One nice aspect of this snake is the fact that its venom is not

particularly virulent. In fact, more than one statistic reports that less than three in every 100 Northern Copperhead bites prove fatal. Reasons for the fatalities that do occur include victims who were heavily drunk, not within reach of any treatment, or simply had a more allergic reaction to the venom than most.

They are extremely easy to care for in

All in all, copperheads are very likely the best venomous snake a hobbyist can own. They are highly attractive, adapt well to captive life, take a wide variety of food items, and their bites rarely cause human deaths. They also seem to accept the company of humans much better than other venomous species. Photo of a Northern Copperhead, *Agkistrodon contortrix mokasen*, by R. T. Zappalorti.

captivity. The climatic requirements involve a dry, rocky terrarium. Provide a large waterbowl and a large, very private hidebox. Their diet is somewhat fascinating, as they will not only take mice and rats almost religiously, but also frogs, toads, and even large insects like cicadas.

This snake averages about two to three feet in length at the maximum, and will be sexually mature in about four years. The normal life span is around 10-12 years. The author recommends that if the reader insists on keeping a venomous snake, then this should most certainly be the one; at the very least, it is a superb "starter" venomous snake.

FEA'S VIPER
Azemiops feae

This is one of the most interesting and

The rare and beautiful Fea's Viper, *Azemiops feae,* first described in 1888, and not kept alive in captivity until a few specimens were collected in northern Burma in 1985. Photo by Paul Freed.

mysterious of all the world's poisonous snakes. Although it was first described in 1888, only two specimens were known until 1935. Keeping with its mystique, Fea's Viper is also somewhat difficult to maintain in captivity, as was learned when three live ones were acquired in 1985 but died soon thereafter (according to some sources however, there are at least half a dozen specimens in North American museums and zoos at present, although none known in private collections).

It is a remarkably attractive creature. It has a beautiful base color of shiny blue-black, with a series of widely spaced thin orange bands that rise from the belly but do not always meet on the spine. The head is also this unique orange, slightly yellow color, and has a distinct cross pattern outlined in a vague, hazy gray. The eye is a little more yellowish, and the pupil is vertical.

Notably, this snake prefers cool climes, and can be found in mountain regions about 2,000 feet up. It is a native of isolated sections of Burma, China, and Tibet. Not too much is known about its breeding habits, and it has obviously not been bred in captivity, but it is believed to be oviparous. It rarely reaches a length of more than three feet, and the few captives that were maintained accepted mice. It is a shame that this calm, beautiful animal is not studied more closely or is more available, as it is both stunning in appearance and a fascinating subject.

GABOON VIPER
Bitis gabonica

One of the most attractive of all venomous species, the Gaboon Viper is fascinating for a couple of reasons. For one, it is one of the "laziest" snakes you could ever hope to find. When it is angered it usually does not even move, but will instead inflate its body and create a hissing noise so loud it sounds like a car tire deflating.

It has what are probably the longest fangs of any venomous serpent, each being somewhere around one and a half inches in

This photo accurately depicts one of the Gaboon Viper's, *Bitis gabonica*, most outstanding traits: the sharply triangulated head. Photo by K. T. Nemuras.

Four representatives of the genus *Bitis*. Clockwise from upper left: *Bitis gabonica*, *Bitis arietans*, *Bitis nasicornis*, *Bitis gabonica rhinoceros*. Photos by R. T. Zappalorti, Jim Merli, Jim Merli, and R. T. Zappalorti, respectively.

length. Fortunately, it does not bite all that often, and would much rather be left alone than strike a human, although it should not be condiered "docile" by any means. Many deaths have been reported.

It has a beautiful base color of dusky or light gray or sometimes lighter (even pinkish or tan), with a lateral series of unique saddles that constitute a mixture of browns, yellows, and blacks, the pattern being slightly reminiscent of many American Indian designs. The head looks very fat and is extremely triangular.

Its native geographic range includes Tanzania, Zimbabwe, Uganda, Gabon, and much of the rest of South and West Africa. It frequents moist, dense wooded areas, although it can sometimes be found foraging around fields during the night hours and is even known to inhabit some swamplands (hence one of its other common names, the "Swampjack").

Its main diet consists

mostly of ground-nesting birds and mice, as it is not terribly arboreal. In time it makes a good, hardy captive, although somewhat unexciting. The average litter size is somewhere around two dozen, although over 50 is not unknown.

EYELASH VIPER
Bothrops schlegeli

Thanks to the budding interest in venomous snakes, one that has become very popular is the Eyelash Viper. This is understandable if you measure the snake by the common keeper's standards: it is very attractive, easy to maintain, and relatively calm.

It comes in a variety of colors (which, no doubt, adds to its commercial appeal), but the most common in captivity is a striking brilliant yellow. It gets its name from the unique network of "horns" above each eye, this consisting of one main horn (not exactly a horn in the traditional sense, and very small), with a series of smaller horns on either side, thus looking like a pair "eyelashes." The eye

Facing page: One of the main reasons the Eyelash Viper, *Bothrops schlegeli*, has become so popular in captivity is because of its vast color variety. Photo of two young by B. Kahl.

Although Eyelash Vipers are not terribly approving of human handling, their bites are supposedly not generally fatal, although they can be quite painful. Photo of *Bothrops schlegeli* by John Iverson.

itself is also most attractive, being a beautifully rich copper color with a vertical pupil.

It is viviparous, giving birth to about a dozen young. These neonates look very much like their parents. The ease with which captive breeding can be executed is another factor that makes them good "pets."

They are native to Mexico, Central America, Venezuela, Ecuador, and Colombia,

BANDED KRAIT
Bungarus fasciatus

Speaking strictly in terms of venom potency, this is one of the deadliest snakes in the world. Famous for a battery of human deaths, the bite of a Banded Krait has been known to claim a life in under 400 seconds.

It is found over much of northeastern India, southern China, Borneo, Java, Sumatra, and the Malayan Peninsula. It prefers grassy, open woodlands, but does not stray far from water very often.

One of its more attractive features is its deceptively simple coloration—a series of straight-edged bands, spaced evenly, consisting of yellow, then black, then yellow, then black, etc., right down to the tip of the tail. There usually is a dark spearpoint on the top of the head and then another thin black band running across the snout through both eyes. The nose itself, however, retains the yellow coloration.

If you are brave enough to attempt keeping one in captivity, and frequent wooded areas near some reliable water source. They are highly arboreal and would appreciate a branch in their large, high tanks, as well as a generous amount of humidity.

give it a dark, secure hidebox and a large waterbowl, and feed it snakes or lizards during the night hours.

MALAYAN PIT VIPER
Calloselasma rhodostoma

A native of Southeast Asia to Sumatra, the Malayan Pit Viper can be found mostly near quiet but sparsely populated areas, including farmlands, overgrown fields, bamboo thickets, and forest regions along the immediate coast. They are primarily nocturnal and feed mostly on mice, a few other small mammals, the occasional lizard, and sometimes even a frog or a toad.

This species is an egglayer and can produce a clutch of about two dozen. The hatchlings, which are rarely over half a foot in length, greatly resemble their parents.

It is an attractive although somewhat subdued species, rarely reaching over two and a half feet. Its base color is a dull grayish brown with a series of large triangular markings covering the dorsal region. These are usually a darker brown, almost pale black color, outlined with a haze of white.

In captivity they like a soft, deep substrate (leaf litter and soil perhaps), with a small waterbowl and a moderate degree of humidity. Their bites are painful, but not usually fatal.

WESTERN DIAMONDBACK RATTLESNAKE
Crotalus atrox

Of the two "diamondback" rattlesnakes—eastern and western—this one most certainly makes the better pet. The Eastern Diamondback, *Crotalus adamanteus*, is considered by many to be the "most dangerous snake in North America," and rightly so. It has an extremely potent venom and virtually no patience for human company.

The Western Diamondback, however, is a little milder, both in poisons and temperament. It is a pretty snake, the base color being a dusty gray with a series of diamond-shaped dorsal markings which sometimes look like they have been "rounded-off."

Facing page: Two of the banded kraits. On the top, *Bungarus fasciatus*, and below, *Bungarus candidus*. These are among the prettiest, and yet deadliest, of all the venomous snakes. They also show a distinct adversity toward captive life. Photos by R. T. Zappalorti and W. Wuster, respectively.

A beautiful example of an adult Western Diamondback Rattlesnake, *Crotalus atrox*. Note the clearly defined diamond-shaped dorsal markings that give it its name. Photo by Ron Everhart.

These markings are first outlined by a fine, hazy white color, then a much darker gray (almost black), and finally a medium gray filling in the center, this gray being darker still than the base. There is a distinct stripe running through the eye from either side of the rostral scale, this stripe also being white, and soft rather than sharp and well-defined. The pupil is dark and, as with all Viperidae, vertical.

C. atrox is an easy captive. It requires warm surroundings, much like its native

will only breed every other year. They are not difficult to breed, however, and at the moment there is a very popular albino strain floating around the hobby.

The young basically resemble their parents in pattern, but the coloration may vary somewhat. This is a very hardy and long-lived snake, some having been recorded up to 25 years old.

TIMBER RATTLESNAKE
Crotalus horridus

Not quite as popular in the hobby as the Western Diamondback, the Timber Rattler is nevertheless a superb captive, as well as a thoroughly interesting snake.

Native from southern New Hampshire down to northern Florida, and west to Minnesota, Nebraska, and Texas, it is a frequenter of rocky, wooded hillsides, nearby fields, meadows, pastures, and dense cane swamps.

It is a very attractive snake in all of its three main color variations. The first has a beautiful straw-yellow base color with a series of thick,

territory (deserts and prairies southeastern from California to Arkansas south to in southern Mexico), and eats small mammals and birds, the former of course being the more preferable.

It bears about 20 young at a time. Some

The Western Diamondback Rattlesnake, *Crotalus atrox*, is one of the most commonly bred rattlers in captivity, and now a beautiful albino variety has appeared. Photo by Ron Everhart.

The eastern cousin of *Crotalus atrox*, the Eastern Diamondback Rattlesnake, *Crotalus adamanteus*, is a much more dangerous snake (probably the most dangerous snake in all of North America), and thus is not as often seen in captivity. Photo by Ron Everhart.

A rare example of what is called a "snowflake" albino, in this case an Eastern Diamondback Rattlesnake, *Crotalus adamanteus*, from Florida. Photo by K. H. Switak.

Facing page: A very brown specimen of the Timber Rattlesnake, *Crotalus horridus*, from Ohio. Photo by Ron Everhart.

dark brown to black, "zigzaggy" crossbands running from the top of the ventrals right over the top and back down again. A second simpler phase is uniformly black and is known somewhat unsurprisingly as the "black phase." Finally, there are some southern and western (Canebrake Rattlesnakes) varieties that have a base color that is more gray with a reddish orange dorsal stripe and chevron-shaped bands rather than simple zigzags, these occasionally being outlined in white. Of course, all of these patterns can vary slightly in their own right, but those are the basic ones.

C. horridus breeds easily enough in captivity, but like many North American pit vipers, particularly those in more temperate zones, it usually does so only once every two years. The young are more or less copies of their parents, except perhaps a little duller in color. They measure just under a foot in length, and the average litter size is between a half and two dozen. They will grow to about four or five feet and weigh up to fifteen pounds.

In captivity, they usually prefer a dry, rocky terrarium with a large waterbowl and a secure hidebox, and will eat mice from day

one. Newborns are not hard to start eating and will live about 15 to 20 years if properly cared for. One final note—their bites, while usually not fatal, can cause extensive tissue damage, and although they are generally very calm, contained creatures, they should nevertheless not be handled unless absolutely necessary.

BLACK MAMBA
Dendroaspis polylepis

Occurring primarily in Kenya but also found in Zaire, Uganda, Angola, Botswana, and parts of Lesotho, the Black Mamba is one of the most feared snakes in its native land—and rightly so, for it is certainly one of the most lethal as well. Furthermore, it is very aggressive and highly nervous, thus the number of human fatalities it can claim responsibility for is astounding.

Its close cousin the Green Mamba, *Dendroaspis virdis*, is much shier, and consequently not as much of a threat. Both are very arboreal and feed primarily on birds and mammals (including eggs and even bats), but the Black has also been

known to take other snakes as well.

Interestingly, the females lay their eggs in termite mounds, a habit that scientists are now finding more and more common in other species as well.

They are too risky to be kept in captivity, and due to their aggressive nature the author suggests that even the most expert keeper avoid them completely.

BOOMSLANG
Dispholidus typus

Although the majority of opisthoglyphs are only mildly venomous at best, the Boomslang is in fact not only dangerous, but deadly. It is one of the quickest, most alert, and certainly most unpredictable snakes in the world.

Occurring exclusively in Africa below the Sahara, it is a diurnal, highly arboreal serpent favoring an environment of dry scrublands, savannah, and wooded areas bordering streams, rivers, and gullies.

Regardless of its deadly potential, Boomslangs reportedly make good captives once they have been given time to adjust to the domestic setting. Their dietary preferences include birds, lizards,

One of the most feared snakes in its native land, the Black Mamba, *Dendroaspis polylepis*, deserves its reputation; it is indeed one of the deadliest snakes in the world. Photo by C. Banks.

Of all the opisthoglyphs, only two are known to be deadly: the Twig Snake or Bird Snake, *Thelotornis kirtlandi*, and the Boomslang, *Dispholidus typus*, pictured above. Photo by R. T. Zappalorti.

frogs, eggs, and small mammals, the latter of which can be offered on a regular basis.

It occurs in a wide variety of colors, but the most common is a beautiful rich green with shades of dark blue to black peppered throughout.

SAW-SCALED VIPER
Echis carinatus

Tony Phelps, author of the book *Poisonous Snakes*, called this animal "the most irascible snake in the world," and by all accounts he is very probably right.

The Saw-scaled Viper gets its name from the sharp, pointed tip of each dorsal scale (most prominent on the lower sides), which is a quality most notable when they are angered and inflate their bodies.

It also has a very toxic venom that has caused a multitude of human fatalities. One of its most alarming features is its habit of burying itself in the sand to the point that only its eyes are uncovered, and then sometimes springs out at unsuspecting passersby. They are wild and alert, and thus extremely dangerous when handled.

Two views of the highly dangerous Saw-scaled Viper, *Echis carinatus*. On the top, a full body shot. Below, a closeup of the sharp scales that give it its common name. Photos by R. T. Zappalorti and Jim Merli, respectively.

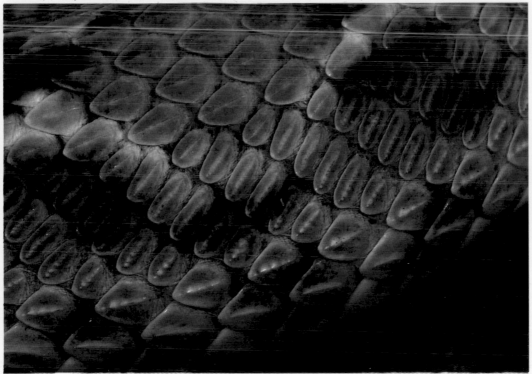

Highly communal, sometimes numbering in the thousands in a very small area, the Saw-scaled Viper lives primarily in eastern Africa to Egypt, and through the Middle East to India, the latter location being a place where they are highly feared. They feed on a variety of items, including mice and lizards, and prefer a warm, sandy terrarium.

YELLOW-LIPPED SEA SNAKE
Laticauda colubrina

For the sake of completeness, the author thought it would be a good idea to make mention of at least one member of the family

It can be found anywhere from shallow pools and swamps to various reefs.

Most notably, it is one of the only sea snakes that does not give birth to live young, but must instead come ashore to lay its eggs. This is a fascinating and perhaps even telltale point that may give some hint as to both the sea snakes' past and/or future evolution. Many consider this animal to be not so much a sea snake, but simply an aquatic krait.

Since they require such problematical surroundings, it seems pointless to go into captive requirements, but it should be known that their venom, although almost never used on a human victim, is highly potent. As mentioned before, they are attractively marked, with the base color being a beautiful shiny gray-silver, with a series of wide black bands.

EASTERN CORAL SNAKE
Micrurus fulvius

There is a very good chance that the standard phrase "red

Hydrophiidae, *Laticauda colubrina*, for no reason other than the fact that it is both interesting and attractive.

The Yellow-lipped Sea Snake occurs primarily off the coast of New Guinea, Fiji, and New Caledonia, north to the Philippines and Japan, over much of Southeast Asia, then to Sri Lanka.

Perhaps it is a shame that the sea snakes are almost impossible to maintain in captivity, since some of them are so remarkably beautiful. Note the flat, rudder-like tail on this Yellow-lipped Sea Snake, *Laticauda colubrina*. Note also the yellow coloration on the snout and labials that give it its common name. Photo by Dr. Sherman A. Minton.

touching yellow can kill a fellow, red touching black, poisons lack" was inspired by the visual relationship between this snake and either the Scarlet Snake, *Cemophora coccinea*, or the Scarlet Kingsnake, *Lampropeltis triangulum elapsoides*, both of which occur sympatrically with *M. fulvius*.

The coral snakes are the only proteroglyphs

For years hobbyists have been entranced by the hypnotic beauty of the tricolored serpents. Most of them do quite well in captivity, but the coral snakes, like this *Micrurus fulvius*, are a different story. These are among the most difficult captives. They usually refuse food and spend virtually all their time underground. Furthermore, most of them are devout snake-eaters. Photo by John Iverson.

occurring in the Americas (there are two separate North American coral snake genera). They are relatives of the kraits and the cobras, and thus highly venomous. However, they are extremely shy and secretive and do not bite all that often (many a small child has picked up this attractive serpent and remained unharmed—although others have not fared so well. Bites are often fatal).

The Eastern Coral Snake occurs in the southeastern corner of the United States, from North Carolina southward and west to eastern Texas in open woodlands and sandy pinelands.

Due to their diet of snakes and their attitude toward domesticity, almost all make horrible captives, refusing to eat and dying shortly after capture.

MONOCLED COBRA
Naja naja kaouthia

Since the rise of venomous snakes as an interesting, if marginal, element in today's herp hobby, one of the more commonly seen species is the Monocled Cobra. Alert and highly intelligent, it is widely available in both normal and striking albino varieties. In its native land—a large portion of the southeastern Asia (including southern China, Burma, and Bangladesh)—it occurs in a wide range of habitats, even towns and cities with heavy human populations.

Its base color is a moderately dark chocolate brown, with a creamy yellow belly invaded sporadically with further brown, slightly lighter than that seen on the dorsum.

As with all other Asian cobras, this one is an

The Monocled Cobra is probably the *Naja* species most often kept in the herp hobby. It can be trained to accept mice exclusively and seems to adapt well to the confines of captivity. Photo by M. J. Cox.

egglayer. It deposits an average clutch of about 10 small, oblong eggs. The young will measure about 8 inches in length.

This particular cobra does fairly well in captivity, although it is still a highly dangerous animal. It prefers mice or rats as its main food.

BLACK-NECKED SPITTING COBRA
Naja nigricollis

Next to the King Cobra, *Ophiophagus hannah*, the Black-necked Spitting Cobra is probably most noted in conversation because of its ability to "spit" venom into the eyes of its aggressors. Of course this is not the only species with the ability to perform this remarkable action, but it probably is the most often seen in captivity.

This skill is indeed intriguing, but also quite dangerous, as it causes intensely painful burning in the eyes and sometimes permanent blindness. What the animal does is raise its head to about three feet, spread its hood, open its mouth slightly, and, by applying muscular pressure to the venom glands, shoot a long, thin stream of venom at the attacker's face, especially the eyes.

Somewhere along the way, an albino specimen of the popular Monocled Cobra, *Naja naja kaouthia*, was discovered and introduced into the herp hobby. Now it is almost as common as the normally colored variety. Photo by M. J. Cox.

Regardless of the fact that most cobras seem to adjust well to domestic situations, they still remain remarkably alert and vicious. Photo of *Naja naja* by R. T. Zappalorti.

Interestingly, if this venom only makes contact with the victim's skin, it will do no harm whatsoever. Don't be misled by this defensive action, though—the Spitting Cobra also packs a mean bite, and will do so if it feels it has to.

It is a somewhat dull,

simply colored snake, being mostly medium brown with a slightly lighter head. The labials are almost white and the "neck," if you want to call the first few anterior ventral scales that, is very yellowish. The eye is round, as is the pupil. It also has an identifying black "ring" around the neck, which is where the name *nigricollis* comes from, this meaning "black collared."

They are oviparous, laying clutches of about one to three dozen. The young will measure about a foot or a little more in length and have their spitting apparatus already intact, so be careful.

They are native to grassy plains, sparsely wooded areas, and some cultivated areas (even where people are working), and live throughout the "rainforest" belt of central Africa. They are largely nocturnal and spend most of their time searching for a wide variety of food items, including small mammals, birds, lizards, eggs, frogs, and fish. The young even grab certain small insects. They are good captives and very long-lived.

TIGER SNAKE
Notechis scutatus

A popular attraction in the zoos of Europe and Australia, many sources claim they have the highest venom yield of any snake in the world. One thing for sure is that they are certainly dangerous and have claimed more than their fair share of human lives. Occurring only in southeastern Australia, the Tiger Snake is a diurnal creature that spends most of its time looking for frogs, but lizards and mice have also been recorded.

Hard to notice in certain surroundings, it is a very dark brown snake with only hints of white or yellow between the scales. The adults rarely reach a length of more than four feet.

Perhaps the most interesting aspect of *N. scutatus* is its unbelievably large litter size—well over 70 is not unusual, and over 100 has been documented on several occasions (but the average is 23). These young measure in

Above: The
Tiger Snake,
*Notechis
scutatus*,
makes a fairly
good captive,
accepting food
regularly and
so forth, but
unfortunately it
also
possesses
some of the
most virulent
venom in the
world. Photo
by C. Banks.

Facing page:
The King
Cobra,
*Ophiophagus
hannah*, has
been called
the most
intelligent
member of the
herpetological
kingdom.
Photo by K. H.
Switak.

at just under one foot and resemble their parents in basically every way.

KING COBRA
Ophiophagus hannah

This is one snake that certainly lives up to its name in many respects. For starters, it is the longest venomous serpent in the world—adults up to 18 feet have been recorded, although around 10 feet is the average.

Many experts believe them to also be the most intelligent of all snakes. If you look at some of the details, there are certainly indications of this. For starters, they are highly advanced in some of their breeding habits. For example, many find a mate and remain with that same one for life, a trait almost no other snakes display.

Their nests and care for their eggs are very advanced as well. The female will lay her eggs in a small depression, then cover it with twigs, branches, leaf litter, etc. She then fasts for two months as she sits on top of the mound and guards it. Occasionally the males will also be present, but this does not occur as much as it was originally believed.

Finally, they have an incredibly virulent venom and can most certainly kill a man with ease. In fact, a full

Facing page:
Pope's Tree
Viper,
*Trimeresurus
popeorum*, is
an attractive
arboreal
species whose
venom is
supposedly
not very
dangerous to
humans.
Photo by A.
van den
Nieuwenhuizen.

dosage of their venom is able to kill over a quarter of a million mice and forty adult males. One even bit and killed an elephant.

They like to haunt savannahs, thickly forested areas, cultivated fields, and swamplands, and usually do not move too far from water. They are native to Asia from India to Indonesia and the Philippines.

Supposedly they do fairly well in captivity, but their main dietary preference is snakes, and it is reportedly somewhat difficult to get them to stray from this. Some zookeepers insist they go so much on scent that they can often be "tricked" into accepting other items, but due to their incredibly deadly potential, the author suggests you do not attempt to keep them in your home, and if you wish to see one, simply travel to your local zoo.

POPE'S TREE VIPER
Trimeresurus popeorum

A most interesting serpent, Pope's Tree Viper (also known as Pope's Pit Viper), although a member of *Trimeresurus*, has a mild venom that is rarely given in large enough quantities per bite to seriously harm a human being. It was named after the noted American herpetologist Clifford H. Pope.

It is found over most of Indonesia, Southeast Asia, northeastern India, and Burma, and is, as you can guess by the name, largely arboreal. It feeds on a diet of both birds and lizards, but will accept the occasional rodent as well.

It is a handsome snake, being uniformly emerald green with a bulbous head that looks slightly "swollen" and consequently too large for its body. The scales on and around the labial region are green with a yellowish tint, and the eye is a striking dark gold with a vertical pupil.

In captivity, it is best kept in a large, very high enclosure. It rarely reaches over 3 feet in length.

WAGLER'S PIT VIPER
Trimeresurus wagleri

One of the particular serpents that has enjoyed a slightly

There are a few color varieties of the stunning Wagler's Pit Viper, *Trimeresurus wagleri*, available to the interested hobbyist. The one depicted here is known to some as the "Kalimantan" phase. Photo by R. D. Bartlett.

increased profile of late is Wagler's Pit Viper. Native to the Philippines, Southeast Asia, and Indonesia, it favors quiet, wooded areas with a dense growth of leafy shrubs, as it is arboreal.

It has a striking yellow and black color pattern that dominates the body (in some localities this black is replaced by a beautiful brilliant green, and the yellow by white), and the solid yellow belly. The head is brilliant yellow mixed with black, with the labials taking up most of the yellows (and occasional white), and the top of the head being the darker. The eye is yellow with a vertical pupil.

A nice point about Wagler's Pit Vipers is that they are sluggish snakes and do not strike often. They appear to do fairly well in captivity although they are slightly susceptible to respiratory infections.

Some workers list this snake in the genus *Tropidolaemus*.

NORTHERN ADDER
Vipera berus

This is the most northerly ranging snake

in the world, even reaching into the Arctic Circle in certain parts of Europe. It is fond of rocky hillsides, meadows, bogs, and moors, plus a wide variety of other habitats as well, so this is indeed a highly adaptable snake. Its geographic range extends from England and Scandinavia over much of Europe through Russia and northern China.

It is one of the most widespread serpents, so it comes as no surprise that there are a large number of color variations. One of the prettiest and most common variations has a base color of lovely frosty white with a vertebral "zigzagging" of very dark brown or black. On the face is a thick dark stripe running from the side of the snout through the eye and onto the anterior sides.

They feed on a variety of items, mostly consisting of lizards, rodents, and ground-dwelling birds. In captivity, they prefer an environment as close to their natural home as possible. They are somewhat difficult to breed, but give birth to about one dozen young.

Can any snake stake a claim in the Arctic Circle? You wouldn't think so, but the Northern Adder, *Vipera berus*, can. It is the most northerly ranging snake in the world. Photo by W. Wuster.

GLOSSARY OF TERMS

Aglyph—Any snake that does not have fangs able to deliver venom through. Commonly used as a synonym for non-venomous species.

Allopatric—Two species or subspecies that do not occur in the same geographic area.

Anterior—The front end.

Antivenin/ Antivenom—An "antidote" used in the hopes of curing the effects of snake venom.

Arboreal—Tree-dwelling.

Caudal—Posterior or rear (tail) end.

Diurnal—Active during the daytime.

Dorsal—The upper surface or "back."

Duvernoy's Gland—The gland that holds and produces the venoms (which are actually modified salivas) in rear-fanged colubrids. It was named after the French anatomist D. M. Duvernoy.

Estivation—An escape from excessive heat or dryness. A "rest" period.

Gangrene—Destruction and ensuing death of skin and muscle tissues.

Hemotoxic—Destroying blood cells and blood-producing organs.

Hemipenes—Paired intromittent (copulatory) organs of a male snake.

Herpetology—The study of reptiles and amphibians.

Hibernation—The inactive period when snakes escape from the cold. This period also triggers the reproductive hormones.

Labial Region—The area on snakes around the mouth.

Lateral—The sides.

Neurotoxic—Destroying or damaging nerve cells.

The Dog-toothed Cat Snake, *Boiga cynodon*, ranges from Burma through Malaya and into the Indonesian Archipelago. It is a rear-fanged bird-eater. Photo by R. D. Bartlett.

Opisthoglyph—A snake that possesses fangs in the rear of its mouth.

Oviparous—Egglaying.

Posterior—Located behind.

Proteroglyph—A snake possessing short, fixed fangs in the front of the mouth.

Shiftbox—A modified hidebox designed to trap venomous snakes for the purpose of cleaning tanks, safely moving dangerous specimens, etc.

Solenoglyph—A snake possessing "hinged" front fangs, which can be tucked into small pockets on either side of the roof of the mouth.

Sympatric—Species that exist within the same geographical range.

Terrestrial—Ground-dwelling.

Vent—The exterior opening of the large intestine; opening of the cloaca in a snake.

Ventral—Underside or belly.

Viviparous—Live-bearing.

Vivarium—Usually used as a synonym for "terrarium" referring to the place where snakes are kept (their "cage"). Means "holding life."

FURTHER SOURCES

Campbell, Jonathan A., and Edmund D. Brodie, Jr. (editors). 1992. *Biology of the Pitvipers*. Selva.

Coborn, John. 1991. *The Atlas of Snakes of the World*. TFH Publications. TS-128.

Frieberg, Marcos, and Jerry G. Walls. 1984. *The World of Venomous Animals*. TFH Publications. H-1068.

Minton, Dr. Sherman A. Jr., and Madge Rutherford Minton. 1969. *Venomous Reptiles*. Charles Scribner's Sons.

Obst, Fritz Jurgen, Klaus Richter, and Udo Jacob. 1988. *The Completely Illustrated Atlas of Reptiles and Amphibians for the Terrarium*. TFH Publications. H-1102.

Phelps, Tony. 1989. *Poisonous Snakes*. Blandford.

Zimmermann, Elke. 1992. *Reptiles and Amphibians, Care–Behavior–Reproduction*. TFH Publications. PS-876.

Detail of a rattlesnake's rattle. Each time a rattler sheds, another rattle segment is produced. Some specimens have been observed with over fifteen of them. Artwork by Richard Cramer.

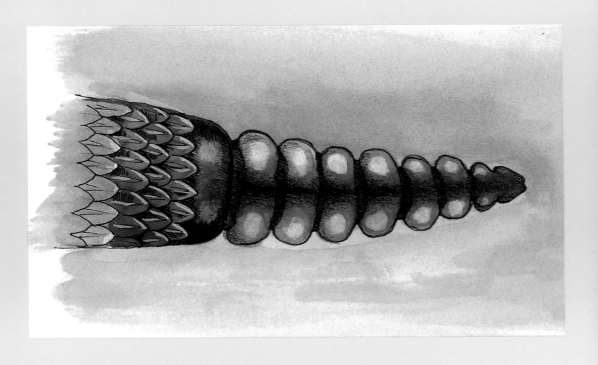

INDEX

*All entries in **bold** refer to illustration or photos.*

Adenosine triphosphatase, 48
Agkistrodon bilineatus taylori, **19, 134**
Agkistrodon contortrix, **48—49, 138, 139, 170, 181** 181—183, **182—183**
Agkistrodon piscivorus, **50, 159, 160**
Agkistrodon sp., **14**
Aspidelaps lubricus, **30 140**
Aspidelaps scutatus, **32**
Astrotia stokesi, **42—43**
Atheris chloroechis, **27**
Atheris squamiger, **66—67, 69, 97, 106—107, 129**
Azemiops feae, 183—185, **184**
Banded Krait, 191—193, **192**
Banded Rock Rattlesnake, **22**
Barrier, plastic, as safety device, **100**
Beaked Sea Snake, **52**
Birds, as a food item, 118
Bitis arietans, **187**
Bitis gabonica, **16, 29, 110,** 185—188, **185, 186**
Bitis gabonica rhinoceros, **26, 186**
Bitis nasicornis, **108, 187**
Bitis peringueyi, **18**
Black Mamba, 202—203, **203**
Black-necked Spitting Cobra, 211—213
Blacktail Rattlesnake, **44—45**
Boiga atriceps, **33**
Boiga cyanea, **23**
Boiga dendrophila, **65, 120—121**
Boiga multomaculata, **12**
Boiga ocellata, **36**
Boomslang, **58,** 203—204, **204**
Bothrops asper, **6, 26**
Bothrops atrox, **145**
Bothrops lateralis, **146—147**
Bothrops schlegeli, **51, 94—95, 109,** 188—191, **189, 190—191**
Boulengerina annulata, **31**
Bungarus candidus, **192**
Bungarus fasciatus, 191—193, **192**
Bungarus multicinctus, **40—41**
Burns, 156—157
Calloselasma rhodostoma, 193
Canebrake Rattlesnake, **202**
Cantil, **134**
Cape Coral Snake, **140**
Causus rhombeatus, **115**
Cerastes cerastes, **10, 137**
Cholinesterase, 47
Chrysopelea ornata, **39**
Colubridae, family, 38—40

Copperhead, **48—49, 138, 139, 170, 181**
Cottonmouth, **50, 159, 160**
Crotalus adamanteus, **103, 198—199, 200**
Crotalus atrox, **171, 173,** 193—197, **194—195, 196—197**
Crotalus horridus, **63,** 132—133, **155—156,** 197—202, **201**
Crotalus horridus atricaudatus, **202**
Crotalus lepidus klauberi, **22**
Crotalus mitchelli, **77,** 166—167
Crotalus molossus, **44—45**
Crotalus ruber, **20—21**
Crotalus viridis oreganus, 168—169
Dendrelaphis pictus, **37**
Dendroaspis polylepis, 202—203, **203**
Desert Horned Viper, **10, 137**
Dispholidus typus, **58,** 203—204, **204**
Duvernoy's gland, 34—35
Eastern Coral Snake, 207—210, **208—209**
Eastern Diamondback Rattlesnake, **103,** 198—199, **200**
Ecdysis, **153,** 154—155
Echis carinatus, **165,** 204—206, **205**
Eggs, of cobra, 136, 137
Elapidae, family, 41
Elapsoidea sundevalli boulengeri, **30**
Enhydrina schistosa, **52**
Eye infections, 153
Eyelash Viper, **51, 94—95, 109,** 188—191, **189, 190—191**
Fang "sheaths", **17**
Fang types, illustration, **25**
Fea's Viper, 183—185, **184**
Fer-de-Lance, **145**
"Fer-de-Lance" Virus, 144—145
Flukes, **150**
Force-feeding, 118
Frogs, as a food item, 114—115
Gaboon Viper, **16, 29, 110,** 185—188, **185, 186**
Geologic time chart, 13
Golden Flying Snake, **39**
Gout, 158
"Grabstick", **75**
Green Cat Snake, **23**
Handling, equipment, 74—75
Health considerations, before breeding, 126—130
Heterodon simus, **36**
Hibernation, 131—135

Homalopsis buccata, **122**
Hyaluronidase, 48
Hydrophiidae, family, 41—43
Hypervitaminosis, 158
King Cobra, **3**, 214—216, **215**
L-amino acid oxidase, 48
Laticauda colubrina, 206—207, **206—207**
Leptodeira septentrionalis, **37**, **128**
Leptodeira septentrionalis septentrionalis, **162—163**
Leptodeira sp., **164**
Linne, Karl von, 19
Malayan Pit Viper, 193
Mangrove Snake, **65**, **120—121**
Many-banded Krait, **40—41**
Mice, as a food item, 108—114
Micrurus dumerili, **13**
Micrurus fulvius, **116—117**, 207—210, **208—209**
Micrurus fulvius tenere, **98—99**
Milking, rattlesnake, **63**
Monocled Cobra, 210—211, **210**, **211**
Mountain Slug Snake, **7**
Naja melanoleuca, **81**
Naja naja, **212**
Naja naja kaouthia, **31**, 210—211, **210**, **211**
Naja naja philippinensis, **54—55**
Naja nigricollis, 211—213
Naja sp., **104**
Naja sumatrana, **78—79**
Northern Adder, 218—219, **219**
Northern Cat-eyed Snake, **162—163**
Northern Copperhead, 181—183, **182—183**
Northern Pacific Rattlesnake, **168—169**
Northern Viper, **59**
Notechis scutatus, **46—47**, 213—214, **214**
Ophiophagus hannah, **3**, 214—216, **215**
Opisthoglyphs, 33—37
Oxybelis fulgidus, **34—35**
Pareas margaritophorus, **7**
Phosphodiesterase, 48
Pope's Tree Viper, **1**, 216, **217**
Probes, sexing, **130**
Proteinases, 48
Proteroglyphs, 29—32
Pug-nosed Pit Viper, **142**
Rats, as a food item, 114
Red Diamond Rattlesnake, **20—21**
Rhombic Night Adder, **115**
Rough-scaled Viper, **66—67**, **69**, **97**, **106—107**, **129**

Roundworms, 152
Russell's Viper, **88—89**, **111**
Saw-scaled Viper, **165**, 204—206, **205**
Sex determination, 130—131
Shield-nosed Cobra, **32**
Sibon nebulata, **119**
Skeleton, cobra, **11**
Skeleton, model, **157**
Skeleton, viper, **28**
Snake charmer, **175**
Snakes, as a food item, 116—118
Solenoglyphs, 24—29
Speckled Rattlesnake, **77**, **166—167**
Stoke's Sea Snake, **42—43**
Tank, homemade, **86**
Tank, "sliding front" style, **84**
Tanks, labelling, **61**, **82**
Tanks, size chart, 84
Tapeworms, 151—152, **151**, **152**
Telescopus semiannulatus, **105**
Tiger Snake, **46—47**, 213—214, **214**
Timber Rattlesnake, **63**, **132—133**, **155—156**, 197—202, **201**
Toads, as a food item, 114—115
Tongs, "zigzag", **75**
Top, for temporary tank, **83**
Top, plastic cover, **85**
Trimeresurus albolabris, **27**
Trimeresurus popeorum, **1**, 216, **217**
Trimeresurus puniceus, **142**
Trimeresurus purpureomaculatus, **131**
Trimeresurus wagleri, **8—9**, **127**, 216—218, **218**
Venom, storage, 64
Venomoids, 75—80
Venomous snake, belt buckle, **177**, **179**
Venomous snake, ceramic model, **176**
Venomous snake, wallet, **177**
Venomous snakes, habitats, **71**, **72**, **73**
Vipera berus, **59**, 218—219, **219**
Vipera russelli, **88—89**, **111**
Vipera xanthina, **15**
Viperidae, family, 43—45
Wagler's Pit Viper, **8—9**, **127**, 216—218, **218**
Western Diamondback Rattlesnake, **171**, **173**, 193—197, **194—195**, **196—197**
Wet/dry season, 131—135
Wound, from copperhead bite, **53**, **57**
Wound, on viper dorsum, **141**
Yellow-jawed Lancehead, **6**
Yellow-lipped Sea Snake, 206—207, **206—207**